"*Illuminations* is a joyous celebration of 'movie mind' —that place in time and space where past and present come together in an instant of recognition set off by a moment in the movies. Pepperman replays the films of his childhood (and our past) today and in his mind's eye theater. A great movie makes visible what, until you behold it, you never knew you always felt and thought. That's what Pepperman's book does for the movies. I loved this book.
 — Robert Gerst, Massachusetts College of Art

"A priceless collection of films and their pivotal moments. Pepperman takes us on an abundant visual journey."
 — Allyson C. Johnson, film editor, *Monsoon Wedding* and *Amelia*

"Great book. Great writing. An act of love—love of movies, life, and art. Pepperman has produced a celebration of glorious moments in film, moments that we relive with him, guided by his gently perceptive eye and meticulous memory. This book is a joyful celebration of the genius and art of sublime films."
 — Tony Levelle, author, *Digital Video Secrets*, and co-author, *Producing with Passion*

"A must read for anyone who's ever fallen in love at the movies. Pepperman recalls these great cinematic moments as if he were thumbing through a beloved family photo album."
 — Nick Basille, director, *American Carny: True Tales from the Circus Sideshow*

"*Illuminations* makes me wax nostalgic for those movie moments that affected my life and choice of career. To this day, when I watch these films, I am transported back to a simpler time, and I remember exactly where I was and how I felt while experiencing one of my favorite pastimes. Pepperman recalls those exquisite movie moments down to their infinite details, illuminating the power of film and why we love movies so much."
 — Rona Edwards, producer, *Killer Hair* and *Out of Sync*, and co-author, *I Liked It, Didn't Love It: Screenplay Development from the Inside Out* and *Maneuvering Film Festivals*

"Pepperman has created a 'movie moment memoir' that illuminates not only the cinematic experiences that shaped his critical and creative approach to film, but also the larger movements in the evolution of movies. It inspired me to take a walk down movie memory lane as I recalled my own formative experiences with film. A rich entry on film history and development that is well worth a read for any filmmaker or film buff."
 — Derek Rydall, screenwriter, author, *I Could've Written a Better Movie than That!* and *There's No Business Like Soul Business*, and founder, *ScriptwriterCentral.com*, *EnlightenedEntertainer.com*.

"*Illuminations* is simultaneously entertaining and educational. It reminds me that the best way to learn filmmaking is to examine great moments in great films."
 — Kazuhiro Soda, Peabody Award–winning director, *Campaign*

"Movies have a magical ability to resonate with our self-concepts. Often a single scene, a character, or even a line of dialogue seems to express who we believe we are. Pepperman's *Illuminations* recalls some of the emblematic moments of cinema that have contributed to our visions of ourselves."

— Neill D. Hicks, author, *Screenwriting 101: The Essential Craft of Feature Film Writing*, *Writing the Action-Adventure Film: The Moment of Truth*, and *Writing the Thriller Film: The Terror Within*

"Combining the wide-eyed wonderment of a movie buff with the super-geek analysis of a film professor, *Illuminations* is a time-coded road map to some of the most memorable scenes in the history of cinema."

— Dean Georgious, information technology manager, William Morris Endeavor Entertainment

"In this moving introduction to those works of cinema that made him the man he is today, Pepperman's reminiscences are a film school in the making."

— Paul Cronin, editor, *On Film-Making: An Introduction to the Craft of the Director* and *Herzog on Herzog*

"Pepperman has a keen sense of what binds us as people, how a great movie moment loosens time's hold on our lives, and why we are drawn to it over and over again."

— Andrea Odezynska, filmmaker, Yara Arts Group, NYC

"In this lyrical memoir, film-editing wizard Richard Pepperman pinpoints the exact frames where, for him, movies became magic. This combo of science and sorcery also returns us to a time when great cinema was as essential to quality of life in New York City as tap water. Read it and fall in love."

— Steven Boone, filmmaker and critic for *Global Comment*

"*Illuminations* takes us on a passage through the classics of the classic, movies that remain unforgettable for all cinema lovers. With Pepperman's detailed and didactic writing, we fully understand the art of storytelling with moving images. Here is a book that every filmmaker must read."

— Cady Abarca, film director

"Reading *Illuminations* makes me excited about films and filmmaking. Beautifully written and wonderfully enthralling, Pepperman's book is a must read for anyone who loves film. His insights give me goose bumps!"

— Julia D'Amico, documentary filmmaker

"n a world of bigger is better, where films are louder, longer, poorly written, and filled with product placements, it's always good to remember where film came from. *Illuminations* is a trip down a cinematic memory lane — a trip everyone should take."

— Matthew Terry, producer, screenwriter, teacher, columnist, *www.hollywoodlitsales.com*

ILLUMINATIONS

MEMORABLE MOVIE MOMENTS

RICHARD D. PEPPERMAN

MICHAEL WIESE PRODUCTIONS

Published by Michael Wiese Productions
12400 Ventura Blvd. #1111
Studio City, CA 91604
(818) 379-8799, (818) 986-3408 (FAX)
mw@mwp.com
www.mwp.com

Cover design by MWP
Cover photograph by Nicoline Patricia Malina
Interior design by William Morosi
Edited by Melanie Mallon
Printed by Sheridan Books, Inc.

Manufactured in the United States of America

Library of Congress Cataloging-in-Publication Data

Pepperman, Richard D.
  Illuminations : memorable movie moments / Richard D. Pepperman
      p. cm.
  Includes bibliographical references and index.
  ISBN 978-1-932907-78-0
1. Motion pictures--Miscellanea. I. Title.
  PN1995.P3947 2010
  791.4302--dc22
                              2010019072

Printed on Recycled Stock

for my mother
Helen Pepperman

CONTENTS

Gathering movie selections for this book established a reflexive addendum to the film registry already in my brain. A billion visions have combined in the storehouse of memory — many amazingly accurate after so many years between viewings; and some unexpectedly false.

— *Richard D. Pepperman*, Film School: How to Watch DVDs and Learn Everything About Filmmaking

ACKNOWLEDGMENTS

I n 2001 Silas H. Rhodes, founder and chairman of the board of trustees at the School of Visual Arts, honored me with a Distinguished Artist/Teacher Award. In 2003 a (more than) last-minute sabbatical request was approved, setting aside concentrated time for me to complete my first book. I now present a most appreciative thank you to SVA President David Rhodes for the generosity of a spring 2009 sabbatical, permitting — at my new older age — an indispensable focus on *this* book.

I have been fortunate to spend Wednesday afternoons at Molly's on Third Avenue with SVA colleagues who provide cheery observations on life, art, politics, and work. I am eager to do right by them, so I'll bet a few fond delicacies — chicken wings, fries, and beef barley soup on me — that Billy, Deborah, Everett, Igor, Jack, Louis, Mark, and Zoran glimpse in this book some smarts resulting from our times together.

Here's an "I owe Lou" (Phillips) for the many emails and telephone calls with ready and helpful ideas that, in one way or another, led me to good-fangled perspectives.

A thank you and good morning go out to Garrison Keillor and crew at the Writer's Almanac (*writersalmanac.publicradio.org*) for a most calming way to begin each day, and for a medley of joy, wisdom, knowledge, and inspiration. And my thanks to Anu Garg's *wordsmith. org* for daily doses of etymological delights and lots of good thoughts.

I thank my son, Christopher, for the many promising leads and chat sessions on the meeting places of memory. He knows a lot because he remembers everything!

Appreciative recognition is due Michael Williams for his professional staying power and skillful rendering of the selected movie frames.

It comes with the terrain as a film editor that I gladly convey collaborative credit: I can give assurance that what the reader holds for study is, in good part (and at times, the best part), made obtainable by the work of the book's editor and designer. Attention cannot be ignored. Thank you, Melanie Mallon and William Morosi.

I have been grateful again and again — and now again — to Michael Wiese Productions for their confidence and approval of my labors: Cheers to Michael Wiese and Ken Lee.

Know what? Cheers to all!

PREFACE

"Memorable," "movie," and "moments" appear to supply a simple initiative. As one might expect, I pulled together my library of tapes and DVDs; I assembled guidebooks with more than 3,000 film entries; I took down *The Complete New Yorker* DVD set from atop my bookshelf and started reading movie reviews beginning with the February 21, 1925, issue; I bought a copy of *The New York Times Guide to the Best 1,000 Movies Ever Made* (doesn't that number put an end to any genuine notion of "best"?); and I purchased Phillip Lopate's *American Movie Critics: An Anthology From the Silents Until Now*.

Before, after, and in between this research, mostly beholden to my brain's seemingly unsystematic incentives, my thoughts, both random and ordered, set off far-fetched glints, mingling movies in abundance as well as, unexpectedly, movie houses, neighborhoods, family, and friends, all scattered athwart time, spinning out windfall memories I'd likely have guessed were nowhere to be found. A totting up of this mélange turned up gobs of stories.

My earliest memories of movie moments had nothing to do with moments in a movie but rather are tied to a memory of my mother getting herself ready. Before I ever knew there was such a thing as a movie, I was alert to the appearance of a young, kind, and overweight woman in my family's ground-floor apartment at 37 Gouverneur Street on the Lower East Side of New York whenever my mother and father were going out. Roberta, I was to learn, was a babysitter, paid in cash to watch my younger sister, Joanie, and me. My parents would often be having dinner at the Pageant Restaurant — a vast Chinese dining hall bounded in miniature black-and-white tiles matched by the checkerboard pattern of its two-story straight-up staircase — and then taking in a movie.

Even for the average moviegoer, going out to the movies way back when prompted a grooming and fashion barely outmatched by that required for weddings, bar mitzvahs, and funerals. Back then, one dressed spiffy for soda and popcorn noshing.

My memory secures how pleasurably my mother prepared for her date with my father, a man who did not enjoy movies: He preferred "going out" as in standing in front of the building for a neighborly chat and a cigarette or two — or more. I can hear his voice with its gravelly roil, safe and sound in the memory of my mind's ear, "Helen! I'm going out for air."

My father, the truck-driving meat packer in his grime-and-stain-soaked cloak, did hearten a finely skilled spruce-up, especially on weekends: He scrubbed and poked his nails spotless, then glossed them with a clear, thick polish. On Saturdays, he always put on a starched white shirt, tie, suit jacket, and fedora, with a gleaming pair of shoes, for nickel-and-dime ante card-playing at the New Era Club's gathering of men on East Broadway. My father did enjoy Chinese food (however unadventurous his menu), so it wasn't too tricky for my mother to have him agree to add a few hours of moviegoing to the dressing up and "Chinese."

Conveniently, the Pageant was directly across from the movie house of choice, the Loews Delancey. It would be years later — long after becoming aware that there was such a thing as a movie — that I would realize the theater chain was pronounced with a single syllable, "Lowz," and not, as my family, including aunts, uncles, and cousins, had thought, "Low-eez."

And so this writing cheered new thinking and old feelings about movies before a single movie moment could become memorable and after a half century of many that did; unfurling folios of memories wholly stimulated in sentiments glued from times recent and long vanished — so many stories still flickering lively.

I am fascinated by the movement on, and of, the screen, the movement which is something like the heaving and swelling of the sea (though I have not yet been to the sea); and which is also something like the light which moves on, and especially beneath, the water. I am seven. I am with my mother, or my aunt.

— James Baldwin, recalling his first movie

INTRODUCTION

My uncle Yankel, an imposing fellow made more intimidating by his childhood pox–scarred cheeks, introduced me to the movies. A letter carrier — Yankel never referred to himself as a mailman — who married the second youngest sibling in my father's family of nine, he and my aunt Becky cherished moviegoing. And so on the day my mother and father accompanied Joanie to the New York Eye and Ear Infirmary for a tonsillectomy, and I was in my uncle's care, he took me to a matinee at another neighborhood Loews. Tickets to the Loews Apollo were sold from an ornate bay booth extended streetside from the lobby. My memory sets a fuzz-of-sorts shot in extreme low angle with a tilt-up to my uncle at the moment of purchase. Practicality makes the case that Uncle Yankel's size necessitated concession-counter foodstuff, and that he would have let me choose something — nibbling from a thin box of Good & Plenty does come to mind.

Before motion picture ratings were requisite or age restrictions applied, when I was six years old, Uncle Yankel took me to the Burt Lancaster, Barbara Stanwyck thriller *Sorry, Wrong Number*.

SORRY, WRONG NUMBER (1948)

"A gripping film version of the classic 22-minute radio play which was made famous by Agnes Moorhead in a tour-de-force performance in 1943. Because Moorehead was not a 'star' in Hollywood, Barbara Stanwyck was given the role in the movie version and she made it her own. [A] wonderful premise which made for a taut... radio play, but at 89 minutes, much of them told in flashback, the suspense ebbs somewhat."

— *movies.tvguide.com*

"A woman, bedridden by an imaginary cardiac condition, who decides to give her husband a call at his office, overhears a couple of men arranging a murder, and then slowly comes to realize that she is due to be the victim of the crime under discussion. Upon this slight framework, an excellent

radio play was constructed by Lucille Fletcher a while back. But in attempt-
ing to expand the network item into a full-length movie, Miss Fletcher has
caused what was once a very taut melodrama to sag rather heavily. As long
as [the movie] concentrates on the doomed heroine waiting hysterically for
the inevitable hand to grab her around the throat, it is an agitating business,
but the adventitious matter that has been introduced into the piece is typical Hollywood shoddy. Instead of being straightforward in its narration, as
was the radio original, the screen version is extravagantly jumbled, full of
so many flashbacks within flashbacks that it is hard to figure out from one
minute to the next precisely where matters stand chronologically."
    — John McCarten, *New Yorker*, September 11, 1948

The *New Yorker* reviewer's critical take on subplot excesses and abundant cross-cutting structures in time could be written as the measure
of most movies and be on target. These problems may be why the
unsophisticated six-year-old me failed to follow the goings-on, and
why bafflement barred my brain from a better chronicling. I have, at
my current age, far less trouble following an entire story, but I am
often distressed that unrestrained subplots and overcutting do serious
harm to so many movies.

    In 1994 I bought a VHS copy of my first movie, which I found by
chance on a sale table at a local video rental shop. I fast-forwarded the
tape to the last scene, and after forty-six years, I watched it again. My
memory of the movie had preserved this single scene. The exactness
astounded me, a result, I'm sure, of the intensely disturbing moment
— my six-year-old senses must have been on full alert.

    Some days later, I watched the entire tape, and that full viewing
confirmed that there were no other memorable moments — nor a
memory of any other moment.

THE *SORRY, WRONG NUMBER* MOMENT: 1:27:09–1:28:09

"Henry! Henry! There's someone coming up the stairs." The bed-
bound Leona's (Stanwyck's) eyes replicate her frantic shout to her
husband on the other end of the telephone line. A view from behind
her left shoulder looks to the bedroom doorway, and we see (as she
does) a shadow cast by a man climbing the foyer stairs. The camera
moves from a front master shot closer and closer to her. The light
that illuminated her face is dimmed by the man's approaching

shadow. She pleads for her life, and her eyes shift slightly downward. A brief glimpse of the fingertips of a glove is ended with a super-rapid pan to screen left, and the camera's forward movement looks out to the nighttime profile of the Queensboro Bridge. The windows of trains passing one behind the other glow in a beadlike string, their rattling clatter barely covering a dreadful scream. The music — an alarm to the ear and atmosphere — abruptly fades, supporting the bridge-crossing trains' reverberations and the customary late-night temperament of the city's finer neighborhood.

It is curious to me now that Stanwyck tussles with the telephone, aligning the receiver to the cradle, the action "concealed" by her eyes, which hold on the killer and focus the audience. Of course, her closing the phone connection sets up Henry's affected (though exciting) call back.

The particulars of the moment's art and craft collaborations have managed to stick in my head; or perhaps they have stuck because of the many first-rate details: the fabric prints on the drapery, headboard, bedding, and Stanwyck's bedclothes. Her hand, in a dying clench, tugs the night table's satin spread, sliding lamp and clock and radio and cigarette box onto the floor, but not the phone — her left hand secures it — nor her framed wedding picture. Finally, her hand slides slowly across the telephone's base and off the screen. The camera moves close on the phone as it begins to ring simultaneous to a harbor vessel's bass blare. A gloved hand "takes" the call. The glove and telephone are not, as usual, of dark values; they are light buff to white. The killer's voice is matter-of-fact: "Sorry, wrong number." The receiver is returned to cradle, and the film fades to its finish.

The year before I saw my first movie, my parents signed on with AT&T, and we got our first telephone. My memory skills were put to the test by my father so that ORegon 7-3049 shindigs inside my skull like lyrics to a popular tune. One babysitting evening when Roberta wasn't watching, I went into my parents' bedroom to try my first outgoing call. I randomly dialed until a voice greeted, "Hello," then plunked the receiver onto its base and stared at it, certain of a looming consequence. So, however awful the terror of my first movie, the killer did contribute a protocol for phoning errors; and I am sure that the proximity in time between joining the Bell System and witnessing poor Barbara Stanwyck assured that the moment would be memorable and undying.

Almost every movie is a fantasy, or a fable, or a fairy tale. In a great movie narrative and technological magic combine to produce heightened intimations of the real, and that ecstatic merging of magic and reality is what imprints the movie on our emotional memory.

— David Denby

ILLUMINATIONS: AN OVERTURE

This overture is a call to the movies, its spirit illumined by novelist Manuel Puig, who, born in a small town in Argentina in 1932, grew up on the grassy plains of the pampas. Puig hated the "total absence of landscape — no trees, no rain, only this grass that grows by itself, which is excellent for cattle, but not for people"; but he did love his town's tiny movie theater, which changed fare every day. After seeing his first movie, *The Bride of Frankenstein*, he went each night at 6:00 p.m. and, from that same seat, saw films by Frank Capra, John Ford, and Alfred Hitchcock. Manuel Puig illustrates the private and public simultaneity of moviegoing and the inspired possibilities that generate new provocations enthused by on-screen spectacle, sensuality, heroics, and then some. Manuel Puig wrote *Kiss of the Spider Woman* (1979), a novel adapted to film, about a gay man in prison who befriends a guerilla soldier with plot-line tales of all the movies he ever saw.

My introduction to the movies in 1948 New York issues this book's arrangements: Selections bring together excerpted retrospective annotations (mostly from *movies.tvguide.com*) with contemporaneous reviews (largely from the *New Yorker* and the *New York Times*). In concert, they present responses and perspectives that are at once historical and (all but) impulsive. An addition to my acknowledgments is due and is best fit here: So much of my pleasurable research was made possible by the extraordinary writing of film reviewers and commentators. I have attempted to arbitrate, challenge, justify, and preserve their observations with flourishes of remembrances in the company of fresh considerations that have come to mind — mine and others'.

I have assembled selections, positioned by the year of a movie's release, under categories: Inspired, Heroic, Disturbing, Spectacle, Sensual, Provocative, Uproarious, Folly, Epoch, and Last Word. These headings are not genre; they embody a determination based on my six decades of moviegoing. They are not what brought me *to* a movie but

how (as best I can) I arrange and explain cinema's influences on me —
what is grasped, grappled with, and cherished *from* the movies.

My selected memorable moments are identified in running time
alone. Changing distributors and the new Blu-ray contribute altered
menus and title chapters to the already available conventional DVDs:
the only constant measure is running time.

Internet and television advertising, along with an array of pocket
technologies, overload and distort perceptions of pure "in the dark"
viewings — a naïveté necessary for faithful memory. I have tried my
best to forget such inducements.

Author and screenwriter William Peter Blatty and director William
Friedkin justified their collaboration in the 1973 horror film *The
Exorcist* by asserting a kind of (self-expedient) public service: "People
go to the movies for three reasons; to laugh, to cry or to be frightened." I think the gentlemen approximate the superficial, not the least
because these words are commercially self-serving, but because they
assume a cause and effect incentive in the vastness of correlation.

The trickeries of movie memories may carry slight or makeshift
glimmers, yet they always affirm film's imposing draw, the adventure
in the outing, and a reflective social history after more than a century
of shared popular culture among families and friends at every age, of
picture watching in the company of lovers and strangers.

Spanish director Victor Erice has said, "When I've finished a film, it's
no longer mine — it belongs to the people." He invites all of us to the
movies, a public pronouncement called in kazoolike rasps: A most plain
woman, unconcerned with style of hair or clothing, toots attention.
She reads from a torn spiral-pad paper that, along with her bobbed
hair, messes in the wind. She is missing most teeth; a few gapped left-
overs are now and then visible as she confidently cries to the town,
"This evening in the town hall, at 5:00, there'll be a special showing of
Frankenstein. Ticket prices will be one peseta for adults and two reales
for children."

Her overture illuminates the instant and lifelong *majesty* discovered
in light beams.

THE SPIRIT OF THE BEEHIVE (1973)

"A haunting atmospheric film that focuses on a young girl's obsession with the Frankenstein monster... after watching the 1931 James Whale-Boris Karloff version. Slow-moving but lyrical, Víctor Erice's stunning feature-film directorial debut carefully re-creates the post-[Spanish] Civil War period... [in this] thought-provoking, highly symbolic work about the isolation engendered by Franco's stultifying reign, made by one of a generation of Spanish filmmakers forced to cloak their political messages in allegory."
— *movies.tvguide.com*

"The film, which arrives today at Film Forum in a new print, was made in 1973, near the end of Franco's dictatorship, at a time when Spanish cinema was just starting to reawaken, and to probe, carefully and hesitantly, the buried traumas of the recent past.... The story that emerges from [the director's] lovely, lovingly considered images is at once lucid and enigmatic, poised between adult longing and childlike eagerness, sorrowful knowledge and startled innocence."
— A. O. Scott, *New York Times*, January 27, 2006

Quick and echoing string beats and composer Luís de Pablo's flute motif escort the opening credits, which are edged with charmingly colored children's drawings of, among other things, a beekeeper with a lot of very busy bees, a calico cat, a steam train, a red toadstool with ladybug black dots, and a gold pocket watch. At the credits' end, a youthful crayoning of a movie screen on stick legs projects a memorable moment from *Frankenstein*: A little girl rests at water's edge. In the grass at her side, yellow flowers bloom. The face of the monster can be spotted in the undergrowth. Some dozen audience members, in widely separated chairs, watch the movie. A zoom gets us closer to the screen, and a title: "*Erase una vez...*" ("Once upon a time...").

A cut takes us to live action, and in a long shot, an old truck drives toward us down the dirt road of a tawny and barren land. A title sits at bottom frame: "Somewhere on the Castilian plain, around 1940...." The truck passes both the right panning camera and a simple sign that announces the village of Hoyuelos. The notes end, and the jangles of motor and chassis and downshift play just above the stillness. The truck vanishes at the next cut.

A long shot gazes down a silent street. To the right is a building in need of repair; its gallant doors suggest public worth. At screen left, two men in caps sit on a bench along a wall. The beeps of an old-style horn initiate the calls of boys: "The movie's coming! The movie's coming!" A group of them dances into view and toward the camera, ahead of the slow-moving truck, which makes a left, revealing a boy who has hitched a ride on the back, and stops at the important doors. Another cut from behind the truck all but fills the frame with gathering children — now a few girls arrive — as men unload film cans and large reels. The children call with enthusiasm, "What's the movie about? Is it a horror movie? Is it a cowboy movie? Are there Indians in it?"

A cigar-munching large man, in a voice all but gone from excessive smoke and tar, entices, "It's a wonderful movie. The best I've ever shown in this town. You can't even imagine. All I can say is Olé!"

Six-year-old Ana watches the movie, allure and trepidation in her eyes as a little girl meets the Frankenstein monster at water's edge and shares flower petals to float on the lake.

Anchored only inches above and behind an audience of old and young, who are seated in household chairs carried to the theater, the projector clatters excessively, its bulb sending illuminations, horizontally cone-shaped over heads; with smokers in attendance, a wriggling blue mist shines through the cone.

Ana is mesmerized and made more inquisitive by her older sister Isabel's teasing tales, including a (made-up) rumor that the monster lives in the abandoned barn that sits on depleted land beyond a single train track. Ana ventures alone to meet the Frankenstein monster. A man is hiding there. He is a fugitive (a member of the maquis, or anti-Francoist resistance) who jumped from a passing train and injured his ankle. Ana offers fruit from her lunch box and returns with a jar of honey, a nearly whole round bread, and her father's well-worn corduroy jacket. Ana attempts to help the man tie his shoe, which barely fits over a bloodied hanky ankle wrap. The fugitive finds Ana's father's pocket watch in the jacket.

THE SPIRIT OF THE BEEHIVE **MOMENT: 1:12:46–1:13:36**

An extreme close-up of the watch as it opens and chimes a pleasant ditty. Ana looks up from her task, and the man, with a bit of presto-magic, makes the watch disappear. Ana's eyes light with a smile, and she returns to the shoe tying. We hear muffled, but clear, the wail of wind, a blowing distinct across tracts of open flatland.

An image illumined across eras, oceans, and cultures, a picture so perfect to the movie's worth, yet privileged — and spirited — in its bond to me, that with neither laughter nor sadness nor fear, I was wobbled.

In an extreme close-up of the shoe, Ana's kind fingers loop the right-side lace into a small vertical "bulb" and do the same with the left before turning that bulb across and through the first to make a bow.

When I was not-quite three years old and too bungling to make a gracefully fluid bow, my mother modified my lace-tying lesson to that two-loop bulb technique, and I caught on at once. To this day, that's how I tie my shoes!

In satisfying synchronicity with my overture selections, critic A. O. Scott contributes: "*The Spirit of the Beehive*, like *Cinema Paradiso*, also takes place at the particular intersection of reality and fantasy defined by youthful moviegoing."

CINEMA PARADISO (1988)

> "*Cinema Paradiso* wallows in nostalgia for a mythic moviegoing past....
> Shot on location in the director's hometown of Bagheria, Sicily,... for the
> folks in this backward hamlet [moviegoing] is as common as going to church
> each week. Indeed, going to the movies is a reverential act, as anyone gazing
> on those rows of rapt faces can tell. They laugh, they cry, they bliss out on
> cue."
>
> — *movies.tvguide.com*

(My *New Yorker* search for a review came up empty, listing the
movie as referenced in "Elements of Film," an article about projectors
and projection booth scenes in movies.)

The entire village turns out for the last day's showing of the 1949
musical comedy *I pompieri di Viggiù*, starring Totò — (full name:
Antonio Griffo Focas Flavio Angelo Ducas Comneno De Curtis di
Bisanzio Gagliardi) — likely the most popular actor in Italian movie
history. The jammed-full movie house bows to everything, from the
usual in public conduct to the utmost in private deeds.

As the camera tracks the theater from end to end, we witness mesmerized patrons in chairs, on benches, and standing along the walls:
Villagers laugh aloud; hold hands with their romantic others; try to be
like Totò, mimicking an orchestra's musical implements with wild hand
and facial gestures. A customer gulps from a basketed bottle of Chianti
classico; a young kerchiefed woman, enjoying the on-screen frivolities,
props the tip of her tit to nurse a soothed baby; a man with a cigarette
in his lips is (no doubt) being caressed between the legs of a woman
who stands in front of him, her dress pulled up and hidden beneath
her coat. As the camera draws full upon them, their pleasure at love
overcomes the projected delights, and the man is enticed to reach out
one hand and cuddle the woman's right breast.

With patrons standing against walls and in aisles, many seated in
chairs carried from home, the Paradiso is more than sold out. Many have
sat through two shows, while an angry overflow crowd insists on another
showing. Father Adelfio, the town priest, aided by two uniformed officers, drives everyone outdoors. "It's late. Be reasonable. We can't have
another show. Tomorrow we'll have another movie. A Western. Word
of honor! Go home to bed." The doors are pressed closed.

The crowd assembles in the town square, and they make their plea to the theater projectionist high above them: "Alfredo, let us in!"

Alfredo reveals insights to his frequent companion, a boy named Salvatore (also a Totò): "'A mob doesn't think. It has a mind of its own.' Spencer Tracy said that in *Fury*."

Alfredo asks the boy, "What do you say? Shall we let the poor devils see the film?"

"Fantastic," says Totò, "but how?" Alfredo laughs. "If you have no faith in me, have faith in what you see."

THE *CINEMA PARADISO* MOMENT: 0:49:38–0:50:54

A close-up of the projector's glass portal begins the moment. Hovering particles are illuminated as if pixie dust were freed by the projector; the filmstrip's image is exposed.

Alfredo's hand reaches from above and takes hold of a pull lever. "Get ready. Abracadabra!" He slowly swings the door outward as the camera pulls back. We pass through walls. The image can still be seen on the theater screen as well, and the camera rack-focuses at the same time that Totò turns to face it. His eyes glow with the magic as he and we watch the moving frames of the feature slide along the projection booth walls and paraphernalia. A master shot brightly backlit with the projector's hot lamp displays a blue soft Alfredo and Totò. And now the moving image slides right and out the uppermost window of the theater, stopping dozens of feet away, across the square, projected onto the side of a building. Totò hurries to watch from the Paradiso window: "Alfredo, it's beautiful."

Someone in the mob spots the image. "Over there! It's the movie!" They chase across the square. Totò shouts, "Bravo, Alfredo!"

Yes! It is the movie!

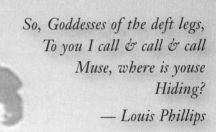

So, Goddesses of the deft legs,
To you I call & call & call
Muse, where is youse
Hiding?
— Louis Phillips

INSPIRED

When Saturday's weather prohibited roller skating down the chancy hills along East River Drive, or games of tag or fence-climbing in Fireman's Park across from Public School 147, my mother would bag a sandwich and snack for me and my sister, and somehow, as only neighborhoods back then could figure, in harmony the other mothers would do the same for our cousins and friends, and we would line up outside the Windsor movie house.

If not for the marquee, one might guess it was a British pub, what with its series of wooden hinged doors, with small framed glass panes painted as red and glossy as could be — and I was well past childhood when I wondered if the name derived from the royal family.

The theater was not, like many of the Loews houses of the day, palace splendid. It was a short and narrow room without a balcony. The floor was ramplike, so steep it guaranteed viewing no matter the height of anyone sitting ahead. The two divides of seats extended so far forward that the first row brought you within two yards of the pro-jected image, perfect for watching the dancing grain across the silver screen and to be intermittently annoyed by latecomers finding stand-ing space in an alcove of tall, seldom quiet radiators, or by bathroom searchers moving far to screen left into an alleylike chamber, which ended in a first-come, first-serve water closet and an emergency exit.

The ticket booth opened well before noon, allowing nearly two hours before lunch need be served. The two quarters my mother tucked safely into my pocket paid admission for my sister and me and for sodas to drink with lunch. The fare, each and every time, was three features, two adventure serial shorts, a newsreel, and twelve cartoons; including what was then called "Coming Attractions," the lineup lasted seven or eight hours!

It did not matter what movie was showing; it was meteorology that brought us.

In due course, the East River Drive served as the setting — a sort of back lot some 3,000 miles from Hollywood — for spur-of-the-moment scenarios inspired by war movies, Westerns, and tales of horror, gangsters, and adventure. All the trappings of a movie's genre were shaped in our neighborhood: A poultry market, fallen tree branches, brambles, and whittled stone gave us primitive weapons for well-feathered Indians.

THE LAST OF THE MOHICANS (1936)

"Arguably the finest film version of James Fenimore Cooper's classic adventure tale, [it] benefits from [the] fine performance of Randolph Scott as Hawkeye.... Packed with excitement and well staged battle scenes, [the] film was masterfully directed by George M. Seitz and magnificently lensed in California's High Sierras by Robert Plank."
— *movies.tvguide.com*

"A few children here and there, satiated with the run of drama and the underworld goings-on, may feel kindly toward [this movie], and the Boy Scouts might endorse the woodlore. When a canoe approaches, you know, beavers flap their tails. However, I feel that the usual impression will be that the studio raked in a collection of the meekest of gentlemen around the precincts, dressed them up like Indians, and told them to make whoopee."
— John C. Mosher, *New Yorker*, September 12, 1936

John Mosher's tone is that of a full-size metropolitan who sat through a crammed-with-kids matinee at the Windsor movie house, surrounded by Lower East Side Cub Scouts as he made his escape *from* the movies.

There have been many adaptations of Cooper's story: two one-reelers in 1911; a 1922 feature-length silent film (by Maurice Toumeur and Clarence Brown); a ten-chapter 1924 serial entitled *Leatherstocking*; a serial in twelve chapters in 1932; a 1947 version produced by Columbia Pictures, *The Last of the Redmen*; and the 1992 feature film in which Michael Mann directed Daniel Day-Lewis as Hawkeye.

While checking out John Ford's *Drums Along the Mohawk* (1939) to see if it too was an adaptation from Cooper — it wasn't — I found that Mosher wrote just as sarcastic a review of Ford's film in the November 11, 1939, issue of the *New Yorker*, upset again by things native and the wilderness. Ironically, on the preceding page was an advertisement for the Boy Scouts of America: "The Camp Fires of New York. When the Dead-End kids want an orange crate campfire they get it! Hard streets — tall buildings — swift traffic — the cop on the beat — nothing discourages them." The images show scraggly kids (in a black-and-white social-journalism photo) standing curbside, warming their hands above a gutter fire in front of patchy brick warehouses with peeling paint, in comparison with a *Saturday Evening Post* look-alike illustration of Boy Scouts in their ranger hats and neckerchiefs, contentedly gathered around a genuine nighttime woodland campfire.

In recalling *The Last of the Mohicans*, my memory of the deaths of Cora (the daughter of British Colonel Munro) and Uncas (the son of Chingachgook and companion to Hawkeye) was only partially accurate, with a juxtaposition that is interestingly archetypal of the eyewitness mind: I recalled that Uncas and Cora *held hands* and leapt to their deaths from a high cliff to escape Magua. In reality, Uncas is battled off the cliff by Magua, and when the dreaded Huron moves to take Cora, she throws herself to her death. At the base of the cliff, Uncas pulls himself to her body, and — in an extreme close-up — he softly *shelters her hand with his own*, then dies.

THE LAST OF THE MOHICANS MOMENT: 1:10:00–1:12:04

Chingachgook calls Magua down from the heights, and they battle with tomahawks and lastly by hand. Major Heyward and Hawkeye watch, not interfering because Chingachgook and Magua "must settle it by their own tribal laws." The fighting men fall into the river from a low rock ledge, and Chingachgook overpowers Magua, thrusting him under water. A full-frame close-up of Chingachgook stages the moment (which I remembered with exactitude for nearly sixty years): straining facial muscles and agitated trembling run downward to Chingachgook's not visible but undoubtedly clenched hands, which grip Magua; blood trickles in a noticeably narrow line, Chingachgook's expression wrapped in water droplets; his muscles then ease (we know that Magua is dead), and Chingachgook exhales, "Uncas."

With this gallant moment in my custody, I asked my mom to save a stocking for me (not leather, but nylon), and I scissored off the top, sewing a small bunched-sausage shaped skein of black hemp across one edge, fabricating a crude cap akin to the scalp of a Huron. I pulled it onto my head, crossed my nose with a stroke of blood-red lipstick, and disappeared into the brush at the edge of the promenade, across the river from the still active Brooklyn Navy Yard.

The movie was far too romantically suggestive for my boyhood and too exaggerated in its musical scoring for me now.

Through much of the 1950s, World War II military surplus was still in great supply — and small demand — and so, as any economics theorist might guess, field jackets and helmets were selling for pennies at a local army and navy shop on Delancey and the Bowery. Friends and cousins disassembled grocery crates, collected broom sticks and old latches from junk shops, and in a few days we all readied look-alike vintage rifles.

A WALK IN THE SUN (1945)

"One of the better films to emerge from the final days of WWII.... Director Lewis Milestone seemed to have put the pacifism of his earlier *All Quiet on the Western Front* on hold. While the film is consistently engaging, some of the narrative devices... such as the voice-over narration and the occasional off-screen singing of a somewhat sappy folk song dedicated to foot soldiers, now seem more of an intrusion on the visuals than a complement."
— *movies.tvguide.com*

"[Director Lewis] Milestone has been aided by a generally superlative cast — a score of speaking actors who play infantrymen credibly. Most impressive is Dana Andrews, who makes the Corporal (here Sergeant) Tyne an intelligent, acute and sensitive leader.... [But the director] from time to time [hands] the sound-track to a singer of heroic ballad-verse... [and] the device does not come off too well, mainly because it encroaches upon the illusion of the literal scene. Mr. Milestone should not have attempted to mix real and expressionistic styles. His picture is most effective when it dramatically documents. However, [the film] is unquestionably one of the fine, sincere pictures about the war."
— Bosley Crowther, *New York Times*, January 12, 1946

"It is only six miles from the Salerno beach where [the film] begins, to the farmhouse where it ends. But out of the adventures of one platoon of fifty-three American soldiers trudging that brief and dusty stretch, the film manages to summon up a good deal more of the sight and smell of war than has been evident for a long time in anything except the documentaries."
— John McCarten, *New Yorker*, January 12, 1946

While the modern digest is critical of the essentially noncinematic use of music and narration, it proposes this failing as applicable in retrospection; yet Bosley Crowther's contemporaneous critique tackles the same defect: The structural, the technical, and consequently the emotional well-being of cinematic storytelling have been century-long matters.

Of all the moments that prompt memories — I am amazed how many the movie holds for me — is an instance that *always* comes to mind, one truly split-second flash. Yet oddly within the war movie genre, and considering my boyhood inclination toward soldiering heroics, the moment is neither grenade explosive nor machine-gun rat-a-tat. It is superbly calm, affectionate, and loving. Perhaps because the moment is so at odds with the apprehension of scheduled events it fixes decisively in my brain: a simple deferment in a time of war.

The soldiers have prepared a plan of attack to take a German-occupied farmhouse. Sergeant Tyne and Archimbeau crouch close to a stone wall. A close-up of Tyne reveals the company of men with bayonets fixed in the screen-right distance; and the close-up of Arch displays more men in the background of screen left. All await whistle signals synchronized to a squad circling the farmhouse via a river and to a smaller squad that will provide covering machine-gun fire seconds before the rest of the platoon goes over the wall. Tyne nearly balances the whistle on his bottom lip. His eyes are closed; he feels ill and fatigued; his helmet embraces his rifle. He opens his eyes, and as he takes the whistle in his left hand, he catches Arch's gaze.

THE *A WALK IN THE SUN* MOMENT: 01:49:10–01:49:12

As the whistle begins its movement back to his lips, Tyne winks to Arch. The wink hardly alters his expression. Arch, in as non-inflected a stare as I've ever seen, in as slow a close of an eye as I'm likely to ever see again, returns the wink.

This not uncommon communication — a silent gesture as readily understood as any idiom between common language speakers — signals neither flirtation nor an amusing retort to insider information. The expression registers a soft regard; a quiet hug; a "good luck" in the face of the platoon's collectively dangerous objective; serene vincibility, unexpected and unfussy.

Inspired games of adventure and war ultimately opened my thoughts to a moviemaking career. As best as I can recall, my initial aspirations integrated veterinarian in the off-season of a major league baseball career — back then, most sports stars needed two jobs. A summertime pal put forward, "We should become philosophers! It's a very good job." He detailed the benefits with highest recommendation: "You get an office with a desk, and a salary of at least $10,000 a year. The boss looks in on you each day and asks if you've thought of something. If you have, you tell him; if not, you say so, and go on thinking."

Despite the allure of $10,000 and an office, I found that filmmakers Ingmar Bergman, Luis Buñuel, Federico Fellini, Jean-Luc Godard, Tony Richardson, and François Truffaut directed my path. In February 1964 — my first week in the movie business — an editor at the Film Center Building introduced me to Morris Engel, the director of the classic American independent (cinema verité) movie *Little Fugitive*. I had seen the film when I was eleven. It is the story of seven-year-old Joey hiding out in Coney Island, tricked into believing that he has killed his older brother.

As it turned out, François Truffaut, director of our next memorable selection, also saw the movie: "Our New Wave would never have come into being if it hadn't been for the young Morris Engel." Inspiration brings new inspiration to blossom, and they in turn turn out even more.

THE 400 BLOWS (1959)

"This extraordinary film was the first feature from François Truffaut, who was, until its release, best known as a hell-raising critic from the journal *Cahiers du Cinema*.... The [title is an] idiomatic French expression for the limit of what anyone can bear.... [Henri] Decae's poetic black-and-white photography... [tenders such images] as a line of schoolboys snaking their way through the streets[, images that] linger like pages from a mental yearbook of school days."
— *movies.tvguide.com*

"Let it be noted without contention that the crest of the flow of recent films from the 'new wave' of young French directors hit these shores yesterday with the arrival at the Fine Arts Theatre of 'The 400 Blows' ('Les Quatre Cents Coups') of François Truffaut."
— Bosley Crowther, *New York Times*, November 15, 1959

"The French film was produced, directed and written (in collaboration with Marcel Moussy) by a young man named François Truffaut, who is almost as capable as Vittorio De Sica at depicting a small boy's confusion when trying to face up to an adult world that is no more enlightened than a jungle. (I'm thinking of 'Bicycle Thief.') The performances are all superior, but in a cast of superb actors, the amateur Jean-Pierre [Leaud] stands out. [The boy is] sent to a juvenile-delinquent home for observation. [He] finally takes off in search of peace and freedom. Running with the strength

of the demented [the boy] finally comes upon the sea, and there M. Truffaut
stops his camera, revealing to us, in one corrosive still-shot, a boy with no
place to go. In fact it could be said that the whole film is corrosive, for it
leaves an etching on the mind that deepens with time."
— John McCarten, *New Yorker*, November 28, 1959

Truffaut's film inspired film critics often eager to cite a school of
cinema as added evidence for personal movie theories; Truffaut, of
course, began as one of them. For me, the film inspired an eagerness
to become a filmmaker and a commitment to valued work.

The movie's protagonist is Antoine. His adolescent mêlée with
parents and teachers is managed with an assist from a friend. Instead
of going to school, they hide their book bags behind a hallway door
and start on a day of enjoyment, beginning, of course, with a couple
of movies: *The Jungle Girl and the Slaver* (1957), starring the sexually pleasing German actress and singer Marion Michael — at the
outset the boys are exiting this show — and then *Terreur a Shanghai*
(1954), with Ruth Roman, Edmond O'Brien, and Richard Jaeckel as
Knuckles Greer.

I know of no one able to ignore the last moment of Truffaut's film:
the freeze-frame close-up of Antoine at the ocean's edge. It is lovely;
it is haunting; it is memorable. It also inspired too many freeze-frame
movie endings. My moment takes in motion as metaphor for Antoine's
unsettled world, and it is irresistible.

THE 400 BLOWS MOMENT: 00:21:36–00:23:58

A high-angle shot aims into… is it a round room? Antoine follows a
young woman. A door, striped with wide bands of white, is held open
by a man in a long overcoat. He has a pencil-line-thin mustache, and
in his mouth is a yet-to-be-smoked cigarette. Several others enter;
the last looks up, waves, and smiles; and the mustache man closes
the door. Antoine alone remains in the film frame. The floor holds
odd-shaped stains, and it and the wall are lined with indications of
segmented portions.

All in all, the appearance of the place is seedy, yet Antoine is
smiling, hands in his checkered coat pockets. He backs more fully
against the wall, and a low-angle cut looks up at five people who are

looking down. A broad gap between the third and fifth makes clear that Antoine's friend is the fourth. A cut back to Antoine begins a lowering of the camera and a turning right spin of the wall. The room is a centrifuge ride (the Rotor); loud voices and shouts of children confirm an amusement park. Ever quicker cranking noises match the quicker spins so that the riders begin to spread their arms, bracing against the pressing energy. With increasing effort and laughter, Antoine, pinned to the whirling wall, feet off the floor, rotates upside down. Then, in an inspiring gem of a shot, the *spectators*, also spinning more and more speedily — in a cut of Antoine's point of view (POV) — are now *upside down*. The moment will forever draw out giggles and a tummy squirm that might only be expected in real-world Rotor riders. The spin slows to a stop and, as if under alcohol's influence, the riders lurch rickety to the exit. The scene exemplifies the sensate command of cinema: a cadenced whirl of a dream dance.

When I was approaching the age of "older," I met Morris Engel once more, this time at his apartment overlooking Central Park in New York City. Though he had no memory of shaking hands with me some thirty-six years earlier, he was glad to chat and discover that a new generation of film students admired his work. I learned that he was a proud survivor of the Normandy landings in June 1944 (Utah Beach), that he practiced free-throw shooting daily at a neighborhood park — he took one hundred foul shots and, on average, hit ninety — and that his handshake grip was as vigorous as that of anyone I'd ever met.

I left his apartment carrying several autographed DVDs of *Little Fugitive* for me and my students, and a new and inspired movie memory. Inspiration is a contagion.

LAWRENCE OF ARABIA (1962)

"David Lean's splendid biography of the enigmatic T. E. Lawrence paints a complex portrait of the desert-loving Englishman who united Arab tribes in battle against the Ottoman Turks during WWI."
— *movies.tvguide.com*

"[The film] is vast, awe-inspiring, beautiful with ever-changing hues, exhausting and barren of humanity.... But, sadly, this bold Sam Spiegel picture lacks the personal magnetism, the haunting strain of mysticism and poetry that we've been thinking all these years would be dominant when a film about Lawrence the mystic and poet was made. It reduces a legendary figure to conventional movie-hero size amidst magnificent and exotic scenery.... The fault is also in the lengthy but surprisingly lusterless dialogue of Robert Bolt's overwritten screenplay. Seldom has so little been said in so many words."
— Bosley Crowther, *New York Times*, December 17, 1962

"T. E. Lawrence was a very odd duck indeed. In real life a tiny man, a bastard, and presumably a homosexual, a self-invented public figure (with a concomitant, and therefore lunatic insistence upon anonymity). Lawrence told the story of his Arabian adventures in *The Seven Pillars of Wisdom*, and his rather high-toned dodging, whenever he reached an awkward home truth, reveals why, whenever Mr. Bolt reaches a similarly awkward point in his script, [director David] Lean immediately turns our attention to the gorgeous desert or to acts of bloody derring-do. In short, a formidably bowwow affair and though tickets to it are so expensive that I feel obliged to mention the subject (up to four-eighty for orchestra seats), I also feel obliged to say they're worth it."

— Brendan Gill, *New Yorker*, December 22, 1962

Paradoxes and contradictions are customary movie review prospects — and with prices approaching five dollars, let's not forget value judgments (and twenty-first-century adjustments). The *New Yorker* and the *Times* critics discuss nearly identical story and character considerations, largely agreeing in their findings, yet Gill responds favorably, while the movie disappointed an expectant Crowther. The database summary — written with decades of hindsight — seems greatly influenced by the film's seven Academy Awards, including Best Picture.

I remember the film in good part because some eight years after its initial release, it was to be re-released, and I was, in a roundabout way, engaged in a practicable effort to arrange a super 8mm cassette and screening device for movie previews. Robert (Bob) Horowitz, a former supervising editor at Screen Gems and, at the time, one of the finest *scanning* editors (better known as "formatting to fit your television"), who had prepared David Lean's epic for its television premiere, was asked to select scenes for a trailer that could be "projected" via a minideck onto a TV monitor enclosed in a black box situated at eye level outside movie houses to attract passersby. I mention this because, though my small contribution had nothing to do with the art of the movie and more to do with the "lusterless" aspects of technology, I did get to see the movie again and again on, and in, various venues.

Following the movie's *entr'acte* (@ 02:23:26), journalist Jackson Bentley turns up and soon joins Major Lawrence and Prince Feisal's army at the time they attack the Turkish railway. Lawrence blows up the tracks, and machine-gun and rifle fire overwhelm the soldiers atop the train, piercing the passenger cars; then the Arabs board the smashed cars and begin looting the bodies and baggage of civilians and soldiers. Lawrence sparkles in the desert sun in his white robe and cape. He is followed closely by a picture-taking Bentley. A wounded Turkish soldier feigning death draws his pistol and shoots Lawrence. It is a hurting graze, with so minor a bleed, high on the shoulder of Lawrence's wholesome robe, as to imitate the tiny bloodletting of a first menstruation — a representation, I suspect, not lost on Lean or Bolt — identified (as well) by a sudden scare, then a titter of fertile delight, fitting to the elegant and beautiful Lawrence, whose cerulean eyes radiate impenetrability ("conceivably" even impregnability) back at the train-greasy and bloody face of the soldier, who fires four shots more, each missing, until Arab tribal leader Auda Abu Tayi slays the Turk with one swoop of his sword. Bentley snaps a photo of Tayi and gets his camera smashed, a superstitious response to the vulnerabilities that "owning" Tayi's image intends. Bentley asks Lawrence for his consent to be photographed, and with hands open, in a near prayer gesture, Lawrence grants the request.

THE *LAWRENCE OF ARABIA* MOMENT: 02:34:27–02:35:31

Strutting an aisle of Arabs who are waving looted objects from train windows to his left and a crowd tailing to his right, Lawrence mounts the car, and to chants of his name and flowing lines of colorful plundered cloths, he dances in a shadow projected onto the desert sand; he spins music-box-doll-like, in part silhouetted by an angelic glow, his body eclipsing the sun. The musical theme spiritually materializes, and Lawrence's androgynous boots "swashbuckle" the train's rooftop. Bentley hurries out from the adoring frenzy and shouts, "Major Lawrence!" Lawrence looks down with a gesture not unlike a pope greeting mass from a Vatican balcony. Bentley grins, "Yes sir, that's my baby," and snaps another photo.

The scene — superficially but commendably — is memorable in its avoidance of black-and-white freeze-frame photo renditions of Bentley's snapshots. Its memory-intensive embrace derives from an integration of audio and images, fully mimicking dream-state representations in the clashing ambiguities of a spiritual and sexual "whodunit." Lawrence as pubescent goddess-warrior? Though Jackson Bentley's last line is anachronistic — the lyric was written more than five years *after* the end of World War I — the song speaks, in a burlesque-vaudeville manner, of the opposite sex; the jubilant photographer might well have added "Showstopper" or "Dream girl" to Lawrence's tribute.

The American journalist featured in the scene, who, via news reports, cheered Lawrence's celebrity, was expectedly inspired by American journalist-adventurer Lowell Thomas, who is quoted by the *New York Times* in his obituary of August 29, 1981, apropos the David Lean project: "They got only two things right, the camels and the sand."

Lawrence of Arabia was re-re-released in 1989 with the addition of some thirty-five (reinstated) minutes. Eventually Lean and editor Anne V. Coates were allowed *their* "fine cut," bringing the movie in at 216 minutes.

AMADEUS (1984)

"The film is a feast for the eyes and ears,... a must for any music lover, any film lover, or anyone who reveres excellence."
— *movies.tvguide.com.*

"From the initial production of Peter Shaffer's [play] at the National Theatre in London in 1979, through all of the refinements that preceded the play's New York premiere in 1980, and now, in the even more extensive rewriting and adjustments made by Mr. Shaffer for [director] Milos Forman's handsome, music-filled screen version, one thing has remained constant and exhilarating:... Mr. Shaffer's ability to celebrate genius."
— Vincent Canby, *New York Times*, September 19, 1984

"The story of a genius who isn't appreciated and dies in poverty has the same basic appeal whether its subject is Stephen Foster or Wolfgang Amadeus Mozart. That's not the kind of story Miloš Forman and the writer Peter Shaffer set out to tell, but it's essentially what they wound up with, and that appeal is probably what saves the movie from being a disaster. What is [the movie] about? Salieri, who has worked hard at his music, been a servile courtier, and achieved fame and high position, is envious of Mozart's incredible talent. You might expect him to ask himself whether he'd want Mozart's talent if Mozart's money troubles went with it, but this movie isn't about such mundane matters."

   — Pauline Kael, *New Yorker*, October 29, 1984

Pauline Kael is (in this) a smarty-pants reviewer seized by ill will. Her questions about the filmmakers' intent and the antagonistic protagonist's (it is, I believe, Antonio Salieri's story) denial of "mundane matters" are by degree irrelevant to story and theme and humdrum in their disdain. Peter Shaffer's play, and film script, pull a little inspiration from Alexander Pushkin's short drama *Motsart i Salyeri* (1830), information I'm certain Kael retains, along with her knowledge to correctly accent the "s" in Miloš. And a slight rephrasing of her disingenuous "confusions" gets to *what the movie is about:* Yes! Salieri envies Mozart's genius — swearing retribution for the Lord's malice, which has bestowed an ear for greatness without bequeathing to him such creative capabilities — but why should *anyone* expect that Salieri would anticipate, let alone evaluate, that God's granting of equivalent talent commands a simultaneous deduction in income or subtraction in status? Shaffer's premise did not suffer Salieri's failure to cast off religion or to contemplate the very existence of the God that so "antagonizes" him, nor his inability to recognize genetic propensities and begin researching — for his own salvation — mechanisms in microbiology that could correct his deficiencies. What would *that* story be about? Shaffer's "celebration of genius" grasps full well the discriminating apprehensions of mediocrity and is a flourishing venture from theater to cinema art: I don't know that any other playwright had ever attempted, let alone achieved, a flashback as quick and determined on the stage as can be expected on celluloid.

   The movie's craftsmanship and grandeur — "a feast for the eyes and ears" — could easily place it under the category Spectacle, but for me, its memorable moment fastens together inspired writing, directing, photography, production design, acting, and editing, in company with Mozart's inspired compositions.

Frau Mozart makes a surprise visit to Salieri. "I've come on behalf of my husband. I've brought you some samples of his work, so that he can be considered for the Royal appointment." No matter Salieri's enticements or offers of refreshment — Roman chestnuts in brandied sugar — from a scalloped gold-trimmed bowl of nippled-breast pastry treats, Frau Mozart cannot leave Wolfgang's manuscripts: "They are all originals!" Salieri opens the leather folder and diffidently places his hand to Wolfgang's pages: "These are originals?"

The *Amadeus* Moment: 00:54:40–00:57:05

An extreme close-up (cutaway, or insert) of Salieri's hand atop the manuscript lures gentle notes that stir Salieri from his chair. He turns (from Frau Mozart), embracing Wolfgang's work as if he himself were about to intone the melodies that flow from inscription to Salieri's mind's ear, and so to the audience. Frau Mozart sneaks another of the capezzoli di Venere (nipples of Venus). Salieri turns to another sheet, and with this gesture, the music changes. "Astounding!" brings us forward to the hospital and the old and wounded Salieri in conversation with the father confessor of an early scene. Mozart's music continues across time. "These were first and only drafts of music. They showed no corrections of any kind." Salieri's words cross back in time. Page after page is turned, and melody after melody changes with them. "He had simply written down music that was already finished in his head. Page after page of it, as if he were just taking dictation." Salieri, in ever-increasing close-ups, appears spellbound, beset by echoes of brilliance. The sweet melodiousness of a Mozart aria arrives. "And music… finished as no music is ever finished. Displace one note… and there would be diminishment. Displace one phrase, and the structure would fall." Salieri's page-turns now enter in slower motion. "Here… was the very voice of God." Salieri glowers, his face framed by clenched hands, as if clutching the bars of a prison cell. "I was staring through the cage of those meticulous ink strokes at an absolute beauty."

A near match, a "gripped" expression, transports us back to the palace and the young Salieri "listening" to Mozart's music. The leather binder slips from one hand, and manuscript pages ruffle to the floor. Two and one-half minutes of ecstasy: "An absolute beauty!" It is impossible for me to screen this sequence and escape the goosebumps galore.

Courage is a quietness, not martial music made.
Born of facing up to life, even when afraid.
— Emily Sargeant Councilman

HEROIC

emory easily holds portraits of actors who eased my many childhood anxieties — illumined even now in black and white — because they measured up to a kindheartedness, proffered in courage, that before movies only the faces of Abraham Lincoln and Eleanor Roosevelt embraced for me.

There was a time when the candy store at the end of Gouverneur Street held a gum and movie-star contraption, and for two pennies in a push-in slot, I eventually got autographed picture cards of my favorites. One of these was introduced to me in the kitchen of the Satin family apartment on Grand Street. Mr. Satin, his wife, two boys, and a girl had come to New York from England following World War II. The oldest son, Noel, was my friend. One day his father took several cans of silent-era reels from a chest of drawers, prepared a 16mm projector, managed open and then unspooled upward a portable sparkly screen. The daylight was made nearly adequate by a tug that closed a pair of blinds.

I can remember the pulsing clatter of the movie projector, made louder by the porcelain kitchen tabletop it stood upon. This would be my first sight of Charlie Chaplin.

THE GOLD RUSH (1925)

"With gags and their overtones of tragedy, their adventures half-absurd, half-realistic, their mythical hero, now a figure of poetry, now a type out of the comic strips, [this movie] represents the height of Chaplin's achievement."

— Edmund Wilson, "The New Chaplin Comedy," *The American Earthquake: A Documentary of the Twenties and Thirties*, 1958

"Charlie Chaplin is in trouble again.... [Six years ago he] engaged a young girl named Lilita McMurray for a minor role in 'The Kid.'... Casting for his newest picture, 'The Gold Rush,' [he has] engaged [the] gifted

little girl (now known as Lita Grey) as his leading woman. And so, last November he entrained suddenly for Guyamus, Mexico, and married her. [This story] was called to the attention of the California Women's Clubs, whose members, fulfilling their obligation to civilization, proceeded to pass some resolutions. [Chaplin] pictures were to be boycotted [and he] was declared leprous and unfit to associate with decent people. Representatives of [the club] went straight to Mr. [Sid] Graumann [sic], proprietor of the most important movie parlors in the Los Angeles district, and told him, in effect, that he would do well to [cancel] the booking [of] 'The Gold Rush' at his Egyptian Theatre. Mr. Graumann, staunch old showman that he is, did well and cancelled the booking."
— "Home Problems in Hollywood," The Talk of the Town, *New Yorker*, March 21, 1925

"What is sure to be of most interest in the films this week to serious scholars and people with background is Charlie Chaplin's 'The Gold Rush,' as he has rearranged it with sound, with a spoken narrative, and with music of his own composition,... first produced in 1925, when Americans traveling to Europe would take a night off from La Scala or the Com die-Française just to enjoy themselves and be beautifully, gratefully homesick at the vision of Chaplin antics."
— John Mosher, *New Yorker*, April 18, 1942

Though Mosher's announcement aims worthwhile regard at Charlie Chaplin's rearrangement, I return here to the original, and silent, movie; except for having a look at my recently purchased two-version DVD set, it is the one I *bear* in mind (a fortuitous allusion to the movie's early bit of dramatic irony as Chaplin strolls the icy edge of a steep ridge, unaware that he is momentarily followed by a bear), and it is the form I hold dear. I offer the Talk of the Town excerpt for its value to film history and tittle-tattle fun. The movie premiered on June 26, 1925, at Grauman's Egyptian Theatre.

Suited in the gesture of his "Little Tramp," Chaplin is identified in the credits here as "The Lone Prospector." The opening few minutes feature adventurous and marching piano, likely a common accompaniment during the silent era, played by Neil Brand, "using melodies from the film's original compilation score by Karli D. Elinor." The first scene depicts heroic spectacle — long lines of men crossing snowy passes in a paraphernalia-laden parade — with stirring titled exposition: "During the Great Gold Rush of Alaska, men in thousands came from all parts of the world. Many were ignorant of the hardships before them, the intense cold, the lack of food — and a journey through regions of ice and snow was a problem that awaited them." I think you'll agree, "was a problem that" impedes "stirring."

The Lone Prospector is snow and wind bound in a small cabin — "The Storm Raged for Days" — with Big Jim McKay, Black Larsen, and a friendly dog. Larsen draws the low card and "must brave the storm" to get food. He leaves with the dog, which is apprehensive about facing the simulated storm of flour and salt propelled by fans.

Though several instances can be chosen to exemplify "Thanksgiving Dinner," I am selecting the entire scene, nearly three minutes, seeing that the exactness in comedy choices and their cadenced achievement hug tight in my memory.

THE GOLD RUSH MOMENT: 0:16:58–0:19:48

Chaplin readies a meal boiling in a hefty pot. The cuisine is his shoe, contributed from the right foot. With concerned care, he tests the tenderness with a two-pronged fork, nudging the outer sole to be extra sure. The trusting Big Jim passes a plate to Chaplin, who, spotting a blemish, tidies it up. And here, in a moment of pure presto chango, tiny thrusts of his left hand extend the plate to an oval platter — just in time to contain the shoe, which Chaplin delivers steaming to the table. In speedy motion he hones a butter knife with the fork, then sits to portion the feast, fiddling his chair a little closer to the meal. With a dash of thoughtfulness, and knife and fork, Chaplin lifts high the shoe's laces as if they were spirals of pasta, settling them on a side saucer. Neatly he parts the "meaty" leather upper, setting it upright on another plate. The full row of nails stab straight up through the outer-sole portion left on Chaplin's platter; he promptly switches plate for platter, and Big Jim — just as fast and much bigger — grabs the platter with the meaty shoe for himself but pays attention to Chaplin, who hones a bit more and bravely starts the dinner.

The Lone Prospector manages the outer sole as if a dish of fish, poultry, and ribs: nibbling, wary of the delicate but dangerous frame of a perch; sucking the last meaty flavor from the nail ribs; and playing wishbone by clasping a nail with his pinky. The shoelaces do indeed

turn out to be an enticing side order of spaghetti — Chaplin twirls his fork with know-how, and downs the dish with dash.

There are instances when Chaplin acknowledges his audience, his persuasive eyes shifting to the camera: "Much tastier than I thought"; "A fine meal after all"; "Oops, some indigestion."

Beside the platter magic is a cutaway to Chaplin's one shoe on and one socked foot, turning from the stove toward the table. This composition covers the fact that the real shoe has been replaced by look-alike, fit-to-be-eaten footwear.

A new look at this film obliges old memories as I (at times) take note of the formerly undetected platter from plate; my old memories of Chaplin have been freshened by brand-new — but just as heroically charming — moments.

HIGH NOON (1952)

> "Not a frame is wasted in this taut, superbly directed, masterfully acted film, the first so-called 'adult Western.' For [Gary] Cooper, this was a *tour de force*, a film wherein his mere presence overwhelms the viewer."
> — *movies.tvguide.com*

> "Every five years or so, somebody — somebody of talent and taste, with a full appreciation of legend and a strong trace of poetry in their soul — scoops up a handful of clichés from the vast lore of Western films and turns them into a thrilling and inspiring work of art in this genre. Such a rare and exciting achievement was placed on exhibition at the Mayfair yesterday.... This tale of a brave and stubborn sheriff in a town full of do-nothings and cowards has the rhythm and roll of a ballad spun in pictorial terms."
> — Bosley Crowther, *New York Times*, July 25, 1952

> "Gary Cooper, who has stalked desperadoes down many a deserted cow-town street, never took a more effective stroll. While the [plot] might seem fairly standard stuff, [the film] is actually a much better Western than we've had of late; indeed, it is a rather rare example of the genre, what with some laudable understatement of the heroic aspects of its protagonist."
> — John McCarten, *New Yorker*, August 2, 1952

All the above are in agreement: *High Noon* is a remarkable work that, with its "fairly standard stuff" — a looming confrontation between good guy and bad guys — straightforwardly attracts exuberant fans of the Western but commands as well the interest of moviegoers who customarily shun cowboys. The choice of Gary Cooper — who was considerably older than his leading lady, Grace Kelly, and was, at the time of filming, suffering the debilitating pain of a bleeding ulcer — confirms Martin Ritt's assertion, "Casting is 90% of a director's job."

Cooper's presence does "overwhelm the viewer" and his "stroll" is so "effective" it does adorn (I might have said "grace") the DVD cover and the disc; and for me, it supplies the movie's requisite memory.

THE *HIGH NOON* MOMENTS

Awaiting the noon train.

0:35:55–0:36:13. Will Kane strolls to the Ramirez Saloon with a few extra tin stars to deputize anyone willing to volunteer to help face the Miller gang. His stride is rhythmically in step with the instrumentation of the film's song "Do Not Forsake Me, Oh My Darlin'." Not a single barroom patron will join him.

0:38:49–0:39:10. Kane strolls to William Fuller's house to ask his help, but Fuller hides inside, having his wife offer the marshal an unconvincing pretext for his absence. Here Kane is accompanied by Tex Ritter singing the theme song, which plays for the next two pre-train-arrival strolls.

0:43:17–0:43:31. Kane strolls away from the camera to the church. Will any member of the congregation join him? No!

0:51:28–0:52:06. A medium close-up of walking boots begins the next stroll, the score more traditionally suspenseful. Voices of playing boys precede their coming into view. They act out a gunfight: "Bang, bang, you're dead, Kane." As the boys run off, Tex Ritter's singing merges with Kane as he pays a visit to his old friend and mentor, former lawman Martin Howe, but with derisive resentment, Howe will not leave his stuffed chair.

0:57:41–0:57:56. Tex Ritter sings as Kane's stroll takes him down the center of the street. Two men evade any exchange and hurry from him.

0:58:51–0:59:39. A POV from inside the Ramirez Saloon: Former deputy Harvey Pell watches Kane approach and pass. This stroll is joined by the player piano refrain from inside the bar. The music continues till a back shot reveals Kane heading toward Todd's livery stable. The accompaniment returns to the instrumentation of the movie's musical theme. Pell follows, and the two battle with fists around and under the stabled horses.

1:03:24–1:03:40. Kane marches — bloody and bruised — to the Ritter ballad, into the barber shop, where he is washed and brushed clean.

1:04:48–1:05:04. Tex Ritter's singing carries Kane past a watch repair shop and to the marshal's office. Kane sits at his desk and writes his last will and testament. Then the marshal and a succession of towns-folk break at the train whistle.

The noon train has arrived in Hadleyville.

1:13:57–1:14:27. A great lift of the camera takes the viewer from Kane's medium shot to a high-angle extreme long shot. Will, now with an extra revolver in his belt, looks here and there down the empty street and bravely strolls away from the camera. Apprehensive melodies intermingle with the Dmitri Tiomkin musical theme.

I did remember from my first viewing — however adult this Western — that Will wins the shootout against the Miller gang, but the movie endures a changed atmosphere in an anticipatory wrap-up as the train pulls into the depot. From here, the structural pacing and actions are so deeply mishmashed to a "new" clichéd score that the movie's genre refinement evaporates in a hurried — though, at the end, happy — final quarter hour.

IKIRU (1952)

"A subtle and moving account of a man who searches for meaning in the final days of his shallow existence. A beautiful and unusually quiet film from one of the world's greatest living directors."
— *movies.tvguide.com*

"For a varied and detailed illustration of middle-class life in contemporary Japan, with a good deal of caustic social comment and extra thick sentiment thrown in, Akira Kurosawa's 'Ikiru' ('To Live'), which opened at the Little Carnegie yesterday, is the best of the series of Japanese films that Thomas J. Brandon has shown at that theatre in the last several weeks. It is also the most expressive in its cinematic style, and if it weren't so confused in its story-telling, it would be one of the major postwar films from Japan. As it stands, it is a strangely fascinating and affecting film, up to a point — that being the point where it consigns its aged hero to the great beyond."
— Bosley Crowther, *New York Times*, January 30, 1960

"[A] Japanese Everyman is inexorably being destroyed by a visceral cancer. Quickly establishing his hero's pathological plight, Mr. Kurosawa proceeds to expatiate upon the sad situation of a humdrum character who has spent thirty years as a minor municipal official and is suddenly

confronted with the fact that his existence has been dismally empty and that
his chances of giving it any significance are slim indeed."
— John McCarten, *New Yorker*, February 13, 1960

Though the movie is reportedly a metaphor for postwar Japan, for me it
corresponds to Ernest Becker's collective writings (*The Birth and Death
of Meaning* and *The Denial of Death*) on the anxieties of mortality: We
are a species — perhaps the only — to be alert to the sureness of our
end, and we eagerly, if not desperately, struggle to secure (for ourselves)
meaning or significance; this truth surely distinguishes human existence.
While the two impressions are not necessarily exclusive, my inadequate
understanding of Japanese cultural history did exempt the first.

Public Affairs (civil service) section chief Kanji Watanabe learns
that he is terminally ill and sets for himself a straightforward task that
calls for heroic doggedness, notwithstanding the all-too-familiar stub-
bornness of municipal officialdom, because, as he confesses to a young
woman coworker who is quitting after one and one-half years on the
job, "No matter how hard I try, I can't remember a thing I've done in
that office over the last thirty years."

He concentrates his last days on ensuring that the Municipal Parks,
Sewer, and Engineering Departments will work together to solve
a local cesspool problem and eventually construct a children's playground on the site. "This is just the sort of matter that Public Affairs
must take the lead on."

The film's structure presents more than ninety minutes of story
time before Watanabe focuses his remaining days; some eighty five
minutes in running time earlier, a group of neighborhood mothers
request assistance: "My child has sensitive skin, and that water gave him
an awful rash." "Plus it breeds mosquitoes like crazy." "And it stinks
besides." "Can't you do something? It would make a great playground
if you filled it in." These pleas are met with instructive runarounds:
"Any proposal for creating a park must go to the Parks Department."
"This really seems to be a question of hygiene. So you'd better try
the Health Department." "Go to the Sanitation Department." "See
Environmental Sanitation." "Department of Prevention." "Infectious
Diseases." "Lots of mosquitoes? That's a job for the Division of Pest
Control." "The problem is seeping waste, which means it's a problem

for Sewerage Waste at City Hall." "Originally, it was a ditch with a road running over it; which means the Road Department." "We're waiting on a decision from City Planning." "Go to Ward Reorganization." "The Fire Department objected to draining that cesspool. There are water pressure problems in that area." I won't bother with the astonishing nonsense from the Fire Department and their suggestion to see "a Child Welfare Committee." Watanabe himself had passed the problem on to the "Engineering Section."

Eventually, the playground is accomplished, and the contrast with the Public Affairs Office — heaps and piles of ignored bundled documents — is substantial.

THE *IKIRU* MOMENT: 2:16:30–2:17:38

A gentle snow falls, and an even gentler song conveys the essence of the film and the lasting significance of Watanabe's life: "Life is brief. Fall in love, maidens. Before the crimson bloom fades from your lips. Before the tides of passion cool within you. For those of you who know no tomorrow."

Watanabe enjoys an agreeable swing.

Akira Kurosawa died on September 6, 1998. He is — without proviso — one of the world's greatest directors.

LA STRADA (1954)

> "Federico Fellini was at the top of his form here, as was his wife and frequent star, Giulietta Masina, whose pantomime... caused her to be dubbed the female Chaplin.... Perhaps the simplest and certainly one of the most powerful of Fellini's films, [it] established his international fame while marking a distinct break from Neorealism in its poetic, and deeply personal imagery (especially the 'Felliniesque' circus motif) and religious symbolism."
> — *movies.tvguide.com*

> "We have no idea why [this film], which won a prize at the 1954 Venice Film Festival, has not been exposed to American audiences until now. Signor Fellini has used his small cast, and, equally important, his camera, with the unmistakable touch of an artist. His vignettes fill his movie with beauty, sadness, humor, and understanding. [*La Strada*] speaks forcefully, poetically, and often movingly in a universal language.
> — A. H. Weiler, *New York Times*, July 17, 1956

Joyfully, the film did arrive in America, even with its inexplicable delay, and it is surprising that the *New Yorker* maintains no review of Fellini's "transitional period's enduring masterwork" from neorealism to "undiscovered artistic territory [which opened] up a bold new era of Italian Cinema."

Strongman Zampanò and Gelsomina, his clown assistant — very much an ill-treated subordinate — travel countryside roads in a canvas-roofed two-wheel truck hitched to the front half of a motorcycle. American actor Anthony Quinn portrays Zampanò, and Gelsomina is played by Fellini's wife, Giulietta Masina: Allusions to silent-era performers are frequent — especially those, such as Buster Keaton, beset by melancholy — as are associations to classic European mime. Take note of Gelsomina's makeup and costumes, especially her selection of hats.

Gelsomina leaves Zampanò after he betrays her (yet again) with another woman — ironically during parish wedding celebrations in a small village they've visited for their road show. Gelsomina might forgive Zampanò if the matter was of infidelity alone, but Zampanò is an everyday bully.

My memorable moment pick will likely appear atypical, what with all the film's illustrious choices, and slightly curious under the Heroic banner. But it recounts an idiosyncratic link to the film, its characters, and Fellini's and Gelsomina's bond to youthful magical woes. The moment illustrates mustering an ability to pull yourself together, to march on, to summon up needed strength in the face of difficulty or distress: Such an accomplishment, with a dignity displayed by compassion, was, for me in childhood, rightly heroic. It is the unambiguous *aide-mémoire* of Charlie Chaplin and, via the conspicuously marvelous eyes of Giulietta Masina, an association to the inquisitive face of Picasso — completed by Gelsomina's horizontally striped shirt, suggesting the Spanish artist and the French mime Marcel Marceau.

Yet, with each viewing of the film, my mind attempts to call up a reminiscent connection that I could almost taste on the tip of my tongue, a mingling of palate and visual cues that for so long have failed to prompt my brain. But now this decades long dwelling is finally secured.

THE *LA STRADA* MOMENT: 0:38:00–0:39:07

Gelsomina marches down a morning-wet road. She stops to rest aside an elevated edging of weeds and sandy soil. Wrapped in an oversize collared cape and modeling an awfully sad Rodin's *Thinker*, she notices a small hole in the slope beside her. It might be the burrow of a small mammal or the hideaway of ground-nesting birds: There is a clear "chirping" sound, but is it from that hole? Gelsomina tweaks small feather-light slivers from the opening, taking pleasure as they are wind-blown from the back of her hand.

As she sadly joins both sides of her cloak against a chill, high-spirited music fades in: Three musicians, each with a different wind instrument, approach in single file along the elevated ledge of the road. Gelsomina cautiously follows; she performs a slow turn and skips with a smile — little twirls dance her into the procession.

This time the identical few instances illumined my mystery: The spin and smile, Masina's vibrant eyes focusing upward — a break from the sorrow — and the skip-hop step let loose (the similarly heroic) Harpo Marx!

When I reached the age of twenty-one, my mother-in-law presented me a gift of a straightforward, though a bit tatty, framed sampler. The needlepoint message, "Dare to do Right" was in red letters on an age-discolored neutral background. That it was from the past came as no surprise — my mother-in-law was an exultant collector — but the inscription baffled me: *dare* to do *right*? To do *wrong* may well be a more reasonable *dare*, however poor the judgment, risking legal penalty or solicitation of misconduct.

How could it be necessary to *dare* to do right?

My mother-in-law, Miriam McClammy, was sixty-four years old and a hometown girl of Wilmington, North Carolina. She was a cofounder of Southerners for Civil Rights and therefore valued the inscription.

It took far fewer years into adulthood than I would have expected for the sampler's plea to be wholly fixed with me: That particular dare is heroic and might be an added category in moviemaking genre.

12 ANGRY MEN (1957)

"Lumet's debut, Rose's adaptation of his television play: verbose, stage-bound, predictable and acted to within an inch of its life."
— *movies.tvguide.com*

"Although cameras have been focused on jurors before, it is difficult to recall a more incisively revealing record of the stuff of which 'peers' can be made than is presented in '12 Angry Men.'... Credit the power of this lucid study to the fact that the attributes, failings, passions and prejudices of these talesmen are as striking and important as the awesome truth that they hold a boy's life in their hands."
— A. H. Weiler, *New York Times*, April 15, 1957

The *TV Guide* movie database is responding to a mannered method of recital that is at once theater and radio and film — portrayals focused with an intensity common to the period to craft an "untreated" authenticity that is, in retrospect, dramatically apparent. The cinematographic fashion of carefully contrasted (black-and-white) values in portraiture also registers the era. Nevertheless, the criticism is excessive, especially in its dismissive tone of 1950s performance design and by ignoring the movie's decisive themes and the heartened courage of the post-World War II decade, which witnessed an immigration of black and brown

Caribbean people — particularly those (already United States citizens) from Puerto Rico.

Weiler "credits" the "power of this lucid study" to "passions and prejudices." Another "awesome truth" — in an era when "awesome" was not the leading responsive adjective — about Reginald Rose's teleplay calls for recognition: the "judicious" revelation that eyewitness testimony is (inadvertently or intentionally) a good deal less unfailing than supposed.

The deliberating jury is at an impasse. Nine have finally decided that reasonable doubt exists, requiring them to return a verdict of "not guilty." Juror 8 (Henry Fonda — who with this film obtained his lone credit as a producer) at the outset was the sole member willing to consider the defendant's innocence and, with an effort beyond what might be expected in a surgical tooth extraction, bit by bit influenced and convinced most of the others. Fonda, in a likeably modest white suit, asks the three holding fast for conviction how they can be so certain. One of them, Juror 4 (E. G. Marshall), presents his thinking about the case, especially the testimony of the single eyewitness to the murder: A woman, across the street from the incident, was finding it difficult to fall asleep and at the very moment of the stabbing happened to glance out her bedroom window to see the defendant kill his father.

The review of the eyewitness testimony re-convinces Juror 12 (Robert Webber) to switch his vote, now back to "guilty." The tally stands 8-4 (for acquittal), though seemingly in deadlock.

The hot New York City summer day in the courthouse has not been made bearable by the single wall-mounted fan in the deliberation room. A heavy downpour does promise a benefit soon; the rain, however, creates an unnerving aural background.

THE *12 ANGRY MEN* MOMENT: 01:23:38–01:28:50

Thinking to set a time limit on any additional arguments, Juror 4 looks up and to screen left to check a wall clock. Adjusting to a more distant view, he removes his glasses — spectacles of a delicate and slight frame — and begins rubbing the sides of his nose, with eyes closed, as if needing a respite before again focusing across the jury room table. The oldest, Juror 9 (Joseph Sweeney) takes serious note and asks, "Don't

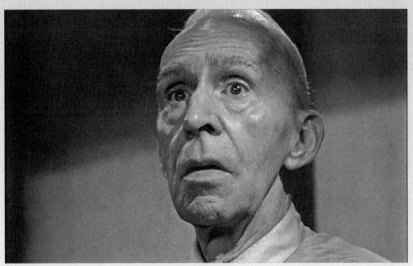

you feel well?" Juror 4 feels "perfectly well, thank you," and again tries to set a limit before accepting that the panel is a "hung jury."

Juror 9 continues his quest: "Your eyeglasses made those two deep impressions on the sides of your nose. That must be annoying."

After receiving an acknowledgement from Juror 4, the "old man" sweetly boasts, "I wouldn't know about that.... I've never worn eyeglasses... 20/20 vision." Juror 9 then gets to the point. "The woman who testified that she saw the killing had those same marks on the sides of her nose."

Juror 4 puts his glasses back on. Juror 9 asks, "Can those marks be made by anything other than eyeglasses?"

"No, they couldn't."

Juror 3 (Lee J. Cobb), who has been fixated on a "guilty" verdict, barks, "What about [the defendant's] lawyer; why didn't he say something?"

Juror 8 (Fonda) justifies the oversight. "There are twelve people in here concentrating on this case. Eleven of us didn't think of it either," and admiringly touches Juror 9's arm.

"Okay," argues Juror 3, "she had marks on her nose, I'm giving you that; from glasses, right? She didn't want to wear them out of the house so people will think she's gorgeous. But! When she saw this kid killing his father, she was in the house alone. That's all."

Juror 8 asks Juror 4, "Do you wear glasses when you go to bed?"

"No, I don't," admits Juror 4. "No one wears eyeglasses to bed."

"How do you know what kind of glasses she wore," desperately battles Juror 3. "Maybe they were sunglasses. Maybe she was farsighted; what do you know about it?"

"I only know," Juror 8 explains, "the woman's eyesight is in question now."

Juror 4 agrees. "I'm convinced. Not guilty."

The calm courage of Juror 8 (Fonda) is persuasive and, from the outset of deliberations, nothing short of daring.

Google the movie's cast and you'll come awfully close to a far-reaching history of theater, radio, television, and film: Henry Fonda, Lee J. Cobb, Ed Begley, E. G. Marshall, Jack Warden, Martin Balsam, John Fiedler, Jack Klugman, Edward Binns, Joseph Sweeney, Robert Webber, and George Voskovec.

Google the film's production crew and you might be "judged" a film buff know-it-all: Sidney Lumet, director; Boris Kaufman, director of photography; Carl Lerner, editor; Reginald Rose, writer; Kenyon Hopkins, music; Robert Markel, art director; James A. Gleason, production sound recorder.

Memories are interpreted like dreams.
— *Leo Longanesi*

DISTURBING

In his book *In the Blink of an Eye: A Perspective on Film Editing*, Walter Murch links dreams to cinema by way of nightmares and unsettling moments in movies. His purpose is to illustrate how uniquely associated are dreams and film. Murch points to the familiar assurance of mothers when their child is awakened in the night, frightened by sleep-state images — "Don't worry, darling, it's only a dream" — and the calming catchphrase when a child is fearful of big-screen happenings: "Don't worry, it's only a movie." Seldom, if ever, will parents offer such explanation for disquieting paintings, books, or music.

I can count on one finger how many times I went to the movies with just my mother in my childhood. She and I went to see *She Wore a Yellow Ribbon* (1949), a classic work of director John Ford. I cannot recall taking satisfaction in the filmmaking craft, but I left the theater disliking John Wayne and intrigued by Native Americans. On another occasion, my entire family went together to a movie: Cinerama's ultra widescreen projection (a 1950s equivalent of IMAX) featuring a roller-coaster ride, mostly spoiled for me by a wide supporting pillar precisely aligned with my seat.

In an era when children and grownups typically went their discrete ways, mothers were seldom on hand as a comfort during scary movie moments, so I sat alone while frightened by images of a man hurled from a city rooftop, a wheelchaired invalid pushed down a long flight of stairs, and other brutalities. I cut back the distress by cupping both hands across my eyes, no help at all for the synchronized resonance of horror in music and sound effects.

Once, when suffering the high fever of measles, I spotted an "assassin" making his way toward my bed, and I cried out. The assassin responded by hiding behind one of my tall toy baskets. My mother hurried from my parents' bedroom, but the imagining was so real that I cried out to her, "Watch out for that man!"

The next morning, Dr. Goldfarb arrived, a genuine old-time general practitioner who made house calls, with a refined leather bag that quartered medicinal vials and syringes that together provided the dreaded shot. The family was assured all would turn out fine as soon as Goldfarb was at the door.

This testimony (about my warning to mother) also establishes that Dr. Freud's ancient theater allegory was not mere hypothesis — and that he too made "calls."

The assassin's attack was so upsetting that I took to sleeping with a United States Navy flashlight, shaped not unlike a periscope, that my father had got hold of while working at the Brooklyn Navy Yard during the war.

Actually, I tried not falling asleep; instead I'd pull the blankets well over my head, forming a pup tent, and click on the flashlight. Either my mom or my dad would later check on me and, finding me fully asleep, click off the light (with this telling, I now realize how the battery life extended through my childhood).

My first distressing movie moments — examples more explicit than the off-camera strangling in *Sorry, Wrong Number* — contain such assortments in killing that by age eight, I had devised a soothing theory (under lighted cover of my blanket) to account for so many dead in gangster and horror movies witnessed at the Windsor. I concocted an amalgamation of the silver screen bodies and the recurrent *Daily News* reporting of the previous night's executions (by electric chair) at Sing Sing Prison in upstate Ossining, New York.

My theory was credible in its harrowing acquiescence to killing, yet reverential in its eagerness to find benevolence in the adult world: all those (realistic) movie deaths were officially authorized executions of convicted murderers who volunteered to be killed as per screenplay demands, rather than in a strapped-in sitting at the penitentiary's death chamber. And! In exchange for the convicts' readiness to die in the achievement of moviemaking, the studio moguls guaranteed their families all the benefits of lifetime care.

PSYCHO (1960)

"Perhaps no other film changed Hollywood's perception of horror so drastically as did *Psycho*.... Though renowned for stories of murder, intrigue, and high adventure, Hitchcock's Hollywood films of the 1950s generally boasted top drawer production values, big stars, picturesque surroundings, and, more often than not, Technicolor.... There's no doubt that it is masterful filmmaking.... One difference [from] the horror films of today is in the age of the characters. There isn't a teenager in sight in [this] classic — a revealing sign of the subsequent evolution of the genre *and* the downward shift in the age of moviegoing audiences."
— *movies.tvguide.com*

"You had better have a pretty strong stomach and be prepared for a couple of grisly shocks when you go to see Alfred Hitchcock's [film], which a great many people are sure to do."
— Bosley Crowther, *New York Times*, June 17, 1960

"We find a dawdling Alfred Hitchcock apparently uncertain just what to do with a young lady who has pinched forty thousand dollars from her employer in order to set her lover easy in his mind about having no cash. While on the lam our heroine stops over at a dreary motel run by a strange young fellow, an odd-ball all right, but his mother, who is concealed throughout the proceedings, and listed with a question mark in the cast of characters, is really far gone. She lurks in a ginger-bread establishment, hard by the motel, and we know little about her except that she is awfully adept at sticking knives in people."
— John McCarten, *New Yorker*, June 25, 1960

Crowther's prediction of audience attendance raises various moviegoing paradoxes: During the silent era, theater owners were concerned that a packed-close get-together of strangers in a darkened room might scare away business, so they paid for orchestration, performed in accord with the flickering pictures. Music, it was believed, would conceal the puttering projector, and most important, it would reduce anxieties, keeping the audience from fleeing. Yet, with all the presumed risk in attending, audiences find extra attraction in fare that promises to add things gruesome. And Bernard Herrmann's score might frighten a radio audience. The "downward shift in the age" of moviegoers might have much to do with television's increasing influences on prolonging adolescent attitudes.

The *New Yorker* query about Hitchcock's uncertainty, "what to do with a young lady," brings up the director's deliberate experiment to see what would happen if the leading lady is killed off early. Punishment following a crime is most often exacted and received contentedly by the audience. The power of storytelling ambivalence is, in this case, accomplished by disclosure that the young lady, Marion Crane (Janet Leigh), has decided to return herself and the money to Phoenix.

As for me, the film stirred purchases of jumbo six-pack bottles of Old Spice to munificently dash on my body — and my waitstaff uniform — during my 1960 summer job at the Flagler Hotel in South Fallsburg, New York, working the dining room for three meals every day, all seven days of each week. The job imposed recurrent scurrying from air-conditioned dining hall to swelteringly sticky kitchen and back again, a kind of "sticky" that exacted a shower a day — and time and again, several more.

When the movie opened in nearby Liberty, New York, a convoy of classic college-student ramshackle automobiles drove to catch the last show of the night, following a hurried after-supper-service cleanup. Showering was, for a shockingly long time, never the same, and for the rest of that summer, taking or even entering one was evaded.

The staff was housed in an extended but narrow outbuilding, situated on double-height cinder blocks, lengthwise along a rear lawn. The rooms (prison-cell small and a bit more raggedy) were aligned on both sides of a long hall and contained a bureau, a chair, and a bunk bed for roommates. At one end of the staff shack were two grungy toilets and showers; no door, no gate, no modest flap for even partial privacy.

Anyone showering — or sitting for relief — at any time of day or night in the wide-open and escape-proof facility fell victim to Norman Bates' mother look-alikes. Wearing granny-gray mop rope on their heads and holding a stick or plunger high in the air, they would race you down while mocking the film composer's violin "screams."

And so I toileted in the refined men's room stalls of the hotel's lobby or nightclub and cloaked the stickiness of the job with flailing shakes of Old Spice's cut-rate bouquet.

THE *PSYCHO* MOMENT: 0:46:24–0:49:03

The silence in the bathroom is exaggerated by the clarity and obviousness of sound effects: the sliding close of the shower curtain and Marion's exhale as she unwraps the unseen but over- (and overly) heard motel bar soap. She looks up to the shower head with a tender smile, her mouth open, the fingers of her left hand reaching cuplike for the water, refreshing our memories of the naked pleasures of overhead water, as if from summer clouds.

I would have allowed the shower some running time so that the heating tank might expel the cool and supply the hot and would probably, during that wait, have unwrapped the soap. But these thoughts come to me only now. I knew, as did every frightened soul in the theater, what fate (and the director) had in the offing for Crane. In light of the potency of dramatic irony — contributed not by Hitchcock but by tittle-tattle — my sensible showering practices meant zip.

Marion's outspread arms and body-soaping self-embraces display the sounds of shower and slow-draining tub. Her delight embodies audience desires. A close-up profile of the "raining" shower head cues two unexpectedly joined images: a medium close-up of Marion's frame-centered face, mouth open to the water, eyes closed, before she pivots, allowing the stream to trace her face; then a cut to a composition that ever-so-slightly looks down in a medium shot. Marion's eyes are open at the incoming frame, but most noticeable is the positioning of her body: she is too far to screen right to keep the clip inconspicuous.

Then it happens! The translucent shower curtain permits a darkening movement to be spotted at screen left. It is a person! The figure and the camera simultaneously approach the curtain, and Marion wanes right and departs the frame. The shadowy woman yanks the curtain across the screen and raises a very long-bladed knife. The sound quickly segues from the fast sliding hooks on the shower rod to the anguished screaming strings of the discordant score.

It took one week to photograph the seventy set-ups that make up the entire shower scene. It takes thirty-two cuts (not stabs) in twenty-four seconds from the opening (of the shower) curtain to the runaway (from the bathroom) "mother."

And though there are a couple of close calls, no bare breasts or knife-cutting wounds are displayed. Crane's helplessly exposed torso, most especially because it is positioned under the continued "spell of rain" (it was, after all, a nightmarish downpour that had encouraged her respite at the Bates Motel), easily and brutally "soaks up" the viewer's receptiveness by way of a collective confidential, illuminating our assumed private doings and secret terrors.

Bathrooms hold close our comfort and cleanliness, a sensual pleasure of sanitary purification. Its amenities encourage a necessary nakedness, an exposure that leaves us vulnerable. Is it a surprise that toileting in untried facilities carries quick apprehension?

It takes another thirty-four seconds for Marion to descend the immaculate tile wall (no mildewed grout at the Bates Motel), reach out to grasp the curtain, tug it off its hooks, and die — her blood diluted into the drain.

The shower scene carries lurid images, mostly as montage, which pry open horrors of soft tissue, imposing a public (and near pubic) display that tests viewer attendance and Hitchcock's restraint to rouse irresistible excitation: many mothers of the day denied their children's pleading to see the movie "twisted" by "that nasty little man."

The dozen stab wounds and the flow of draining blood does not equal, for me, the manifestly disturbing "attack" of the head and face — even lacking explicit wounds or death. It is the face into which the brain situates; the face that "spots" us and reaches four (and more) of

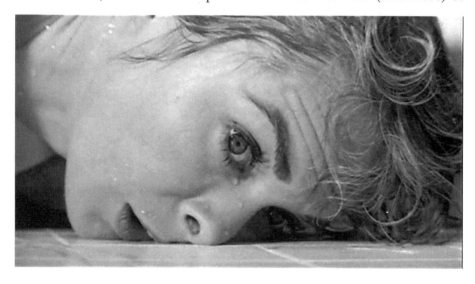

our senses. The face is so efficiently intimate with, and to, our minds
and thus to all notions of self — an urn to memory, current thought,
and the charting of next moments — instantly chary of ever-shifting
exteriors and their enticements. We may distinguish ourselves by
strolling upright on legs and lugging tools in hand, but endangering
the face risks the survival of recognition: It is how we are remembered.

Z (1969)

"Originally subtitled "The Anatomy of a Political Assassination," this
intense political thriller is based on the real-life 1963 killing of Gregorios
Lambrakis, a Greek liberal whose extreme popularity and advocacy of
peace shook the stability of the government in power.... At the Cannes
Film Festival it received a unanimous vote for the Jury Prize, [and it took]
Oscars for Best Foreign Film and Best Editing.... The score is by Mikis
Theodorakis — who was under arrest in Greece at the time."
— *movies.tvguide.com*

"Costa-Gavras's French film is an immensely entertaining movie — a
topical melodrama that manipulates our emotional responses and appeals to
our best prejudices in such satisfying ways that it is likely to be mistaken as
a work of fine — rather than popular — movie art. The film, which opened
at the Beekman, is based on Vassilis Vassilikos's novel, which, in turn, is a
lightly fictionalized account of the assassination in Salonika of Gregarios
Lambrakis, a professor of medicine at the University of Athens and a leader
of the forces opposing the placement of Polaris missiles in Greece."
— Vincent Canby, *New York Times*, December 9, 1969

"[The film] is almost intolerably exciting — a political thriller that
builds up so much tension that you'll probably feel all knotted up by the
time it's over.... The pace and staccato editing, the strong sense of forward
movement in the storytelling [keep the audience] under pressure. The
young director Costa-Gavras, using everything he knows to drive home his
points as effectively as possible, has made something unusual in European
films — a political film with a purpose, and at the same time, a thoroughly
commercial film. It derives not from the traditions of the French film, but
from American gangster movies and prison pictures. [The movie] could not
be made in Salonika; it was shot in Algeria in French. Costa-Gavras was a
leading ballet dancer in Greece before going to France, where he studied
filmmaking. [He is currently] a Greek exile."
— Pauline Kael, *New Yorker*, December 13, 1969

The *TV Guide* database and Kael both — in their full reviews — express the movie's exhilarating ride by referencing a roller coaster. Others have mentioned "knock your socks off" and "knock you out of your seat," or at least, "finding yourself on the edge of your seat." The movie did — if I'm permitted a cliché (or two) — open wounds and touch a few raw nerves by its inescapable correspondence to the Kennedy and King assassinations.

On the DVD, chapter 19, entitled "The Widow," is more than a foreshadowing if you glance at the selections before pressing "play" — it is less a tension-builder than a giveaway, not unlike asking a friend if she's heard a joke by referencing the punchline. It does harm because it purges all tension over whether The Deputy will survive the brutal attack and the conspiracy against him.

The recklessly overt act of violence may make it the most apparent movie moment — memorable and disturbing — but I offer a scene by proportion more tranquil, an instance oddly serene yet equally upsetting.

The Deputy's wife, Helene, arrives at the hospital surrounded by her husband's aides and a swarming press. Flashbacks of memories that are "touching" and expository are boldly launched during the "now" of the lobby and the elevator ride.

THE Z MOMENT: 0:49:28–0:49:51

A doctor escorts Helene. Policemen guard a foyer and an open door-way. Upon entering, the aides stop at a large glass partition between the hall and a conference room. A small gesture by the doctor invites Helene to enter the doorway. The movements create a medium close-up from the initial long shot. Helene's eyes make known her interest in the room ahead. We can hear a man's voice: "The fall broke the dome of the skull... and no doubt the brain has been affected. The shock was very violent... causing an explosion inside the skull like an earthquake."

The last line "follows" Helene into the room as the camera pans right, across a background of books, coming to rest behind her. Uniformed military and police and government officials stand — their backs to Helene and us — listening to the voice of a white-coated doctor. A lighted wall of head x-rays illustrates the doctor's report, but

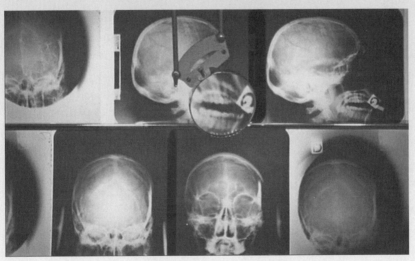

when the next cut brings us face to face with Helene, we no longer listen to the diagnosis — her restrained facial tremors and the awful sadness in her eyes effectively cut off all sound. Then we are again behind the men for but a split second: A dizzying zoom brings us to the wall of light and skull images. One image emerges as a pulley-rigged arm clasps a magnifying lens at teeth level on the skull, provoking a distortion that singles out one of the multiple faces. It distresses with a chilling detachment and the context of the moment: an inspection by outsiders — some of them deadly foes — that breaches any compassion, with the next close-up of Helene conveying the perilous setting and threatening prospects.

That Costa-Gavras had been a leading ballet dancer before studying filmmaking should come not only as no surprise but as an aha! There is, I am persuaded, a more essential and imposing bond between film and dance (and music) than there is — no matter the comfortable assumptions — between film and literature and theater. Costa-Gavras' complex maneuverings of camera and character (let alone his command of crowded chaos) is luminous ballet.

THE EXORCIST (1973)

"[The film] shrewdly exploits the fears and frustrations of parents while disturbing religious implications merely provide portentous window dressing."
— *movies.tvguide.com*

"The book turns up on high school reading lists now, and the Bantam edition carries such quotes as, 'Deeply religious... a parable for our times' and 'The Exorcist should be read twice; the first time for the passion and horrifying intensity of the story, with a second reading to savor the subtleties of language and phrasing overlooked in the mounting excitement of the first perusal. As a movie 'The Exorcist' is too ugly a phenomenon to take lightly."
— Pauline Kael, *New Yorker*, January 7, 1974

"A chunk of elegant occultist claptrap that opened yesterday at the Cinema I, . . . it establishes a new low for grotesque special effects [that], I assume, have some sort of religious approval since two Jesuit priests, who are listed among the film's technical advisers, also appear in the film as actors.... Not an unintelligently put-together film, which makes one all the more impatient with it. The producer and director have gone whole hog on (and over) their budget, which included the financing of a location trip to Iraq to shoot a lovely, eerie prefatory sequence at an archeological dig that is, as far as I can see, not especially essential to the business that comes after."
— Vincent Canby, *New York Times*, December 27, 1973

The film suffers serious harm from so many subplots — the dig in Iraq is only one of a dozen or so, and it is at least "lovely" and "eerie" — that almost certainly aren't essential even in the novel and are harsh and merciless in the movie. Many of the subplots swell into add-on subplots so that the creditable story takes close to fifty minutes to get under way.

Several moments, in image and language, frame the most memorable: the thick green bile (split-pea soup) heaves; the 360-degree head spin; the insolent omen and public urination at the Georgetown party; and the many explicit "suggestions" from twelve-year-old Regan in deathly guttural intonations. As for me, the scenes of high-tech ghoulish modern medicine are the most disturbingly unforgettable.

Jerome Groopman, M.D., in his book *How Doctors Think*, attends to the frustrations and fears Regan's mother, Mrs. McNeil, would be expected to endure in a real-life situation.

However fanciful the film's "demonic diagnosis" (conveyed by Fathers Merrin and Karras), too many M.D.s hear a patient's complaint with marginal "listening" and reckon the case solved (usually) in as little as *twenty seconds:* A fiercely bouncing bed is, to the movie's Dr. Klein, the result of a lesion in Regan's temporal lobe. The doctor orders tests!

Here is a moment, in meticulous authenticity, that transforms a monitored blood flow from Regan into an unrestricted cringe.

THE EXORCIST MOMENT: 0:49:50–0:51:34

Viewing the top of Regan's head, the camera is positioned at the end of an exam table. A technician enters at screen right and activates the motorized platform, bringing Regan closer to him and away from the camera. The tidy calm of the medical technology is stressed, though not without a trace of menace, by the sound of the machinery that glides this table-bed: No violent bouncing here. It is a long slow ride, time enough for a blood-pressure cuff to be wrapped onto Regan's right arm. An unpleasantly tinted rubber mat, with half-dollar size holes, is tucked under her head and shoulders. Her hospital robe is opened, and with assistance, it becomes a bare-shouldered gown, tucked in just above Regan's breasts. Electrodes are joined to each shoulder. Comforting words are lucid above the ceaseless whir in the room. A gauze pad, soaked in a yellowish rust-colored antiseptic, is brushed generously onto the right side of Regan's neck. A close-up of a syringe and its test spew refocuses to a medium long shot of observers overhead: Dr. Klein, a technician, and Mrs. McNeil.

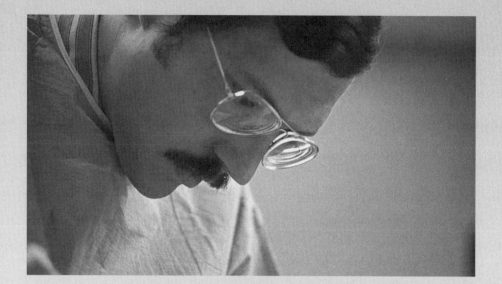

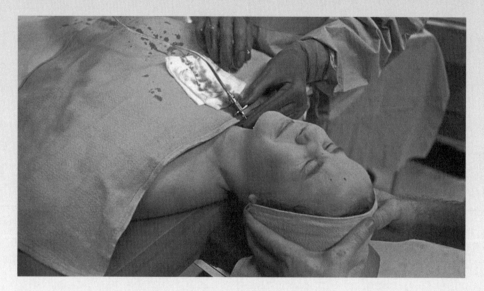

A needle stick that we don't see enters the cleansed neck area, and a stainless steel tube is inserted into the fresh channel of a vein; this too is not shown but is effective nonetheless, with Regan's grimace and whimper and Mrs. McNeil's apprehensive reaction. Then, in an above-angle medium shot, the technician's brown gloved hand lifts a small cap on the tube and deep red blood squirts every which way, staining gauze pads atop the light blue surgical blanket that covers Regan. The blanket too is blood splattered as the technician adroitly introduces clear hollow plastic onto the stainless tubing. Instantly, blood fills the plastic, moving upward from Regan's neck. A broad piece of surgical tape is placed across her chin to hold her head steady. The procedure will impart scanned images of Regan's brain, sustained by infused dye.

I suspect that the disquieting, if not nauseating, sensation at the sight of first blood — there is a restrained wretch with the imagined insertions — is genetically encoded and offers survivability to our species: Escaping blood succeeds in getting our attention, generating sudden feelings of queasiness and frailty, so disturbing that we will not ignore the seepage. While we may, with experience and age, overcome initially intense squeamishness, we are predisposed to "fix things" at the first sign of wounding. The puncture and bloodletting likely exploit ancestral memories.

CHINATOWN (1974)

"A wonderfully brooding, suspenseful revisitation of the land of film noir, [the movie] is not only one of the greatest detective films, but one of the most perfectly constructed of all films.... [It] stands as one of the best of the 1970s."
— *movies.tvguide.com*

"[The movie] is something of a test for the writer who comes after Dashiell Hammett and Raymond Chandler and who doesn't hesitate to evoke their memories and thus invite comparison. Robert Towne... is good but I'm not sure he's good enough to compete with the big boys.... Mr. Polanski himself turns up in the film's most vicious scene, playing the half-pint hood who neatly slices one of J. J. Gittes's nostrils, thus requiring the detective to go through the rest of the picture with stitches that look like blood-encrusted cat's whiskers sticking out of his nose."
— Vincent Canby, *New York Times*, June 21, 1974

" [A] throwback to all those private-eye movies, often based on novels by Dashiell Hammet or Raymond Chandler, that supplied the cinema of our formative years (or merely impressionable years) with one of its juiciest genres. The plot could hardly be more archetypal. So what is new about [the film]? What primarily distinguishes [it] from its models is the new sensibility of the director and scenarist, and the new technology, wide-screen and color, which interestingly distort the old simplicities. But what really brings the film into the 1970s is the loss of innocence that permeates its world: the boundaries between right and wrong have become hazy even in the good — or better — people, and the two genuine innocents of the film are both, in one way or another, victimized."
— John Simon, "Jaundice of the Soul," *Reverse Angle: A Decade of American Films* (1982)

"[S]et in the thirties, the film is wickedly skillful, funny and socially alert. Like Hitchcock, Polanski can spring a non-happening on one which is as frightening as anything that happens. Because of its emphasis on greed, [the film] is a thriller for grown-ups."
— Penelope Gilliatt, *New Yorker*, July 1, 1974

As is often the case, individual responsiveness can be all over the place. A critic's inclination to offer comparisons — favorable or not — of writers, directors, cinematographers, editors, actors, and (in this case) the effects of filmmaking tools on genre earns the enticement of a look back, though, as often as not, retrospective comments afford judgments no more insightful than those contemporaneous.

Private detective Jake Gittes confronts water allocation and associated financial and political power in Depression-era Southern California. At dusk he drives up to the "No Trespassing" gate of a Los Angeles city reservoir and climbs the fence. No sooner does he begin to snoop about when two blasts, very much the sounds of rifle fire, have him scrambling for cover in a cement aqueduct. The prolonged reverberation of the last "gunshot" nearly segues into a rattlelike pumping noise, followed by the sound and sight of speeding water. Jake is flushed to an inner fence, which he scales, minus one "Goddamn Florsheim shoe."

THE *CHINATOWN* MOMENT: 0:42:10–0:42:43

As Gittes is about to climb the perimeter fence to return to his car, a voice calls out, "Hold it there, kitty cat!" Two men approach. Jake refers to them as "Claude" and "the midget." The midget pulls a switchblade knife, and the bulky Claude quick punches Jake in the gut, then restrains him from behind. The midget dispenses a scolding: "You're a very nosy fellow, kitty cat, huh? You know what happens to nosy fellows?" slipping the tip of the blade inside Jake's left nostril. "Huh, no? Want to guess? Huh, no? Okay. They lose their noses." A nasty swipe opens the nostril; blood squirts onto Jake's face and into his cupped hand. The slice sets off an unpreventable wince.

The wounding of the snooping, now sopping, Gittes is particularly unsettling — a Freudian symbol of castration notwithstanding — as it damages the face and therefore both public and privileged identity as well as a sensory function indispensable for a private eye. Depicting Jake's stitches as looking "like blood-encrusted cat's whiskers" might have come to Canby with the midget's, "Hold it there, kitty cat!"

Roman Polanski's appearance — in a white suit and tidy Panama hat — makes the moment memorable if only in celebrity and criminal histories long past and immediate.

MARATHON MAN (1976)

> "A truly harrowing film, *Marathon Man* is a clever series of accidents that produce a nightmare thriller with an unrelenting attack on the viewer's nerves."
> — *movies.tvguide.com*

> "[A] project that seemed a lead pipe cinch to be the kind of visceral thriller that makes audiences almost sick with excitement has fouled up right from the word go. Instead of setting up the situation, director John Schlesinger opts for so much frazzled cross-cutting that there's no suspense. There isn't the clarity for suspense."
> — Pauline Kael, *New Yorker*, October 11, 1976

A simplicity — or "clarity" — would require staying focused on the central plot premise: A Nazi, long in hiding in South America, arrives in New York City to secure riches in diamonds stolen from Jewish concentration camp victims.

The "frazzled cross-cutting," and thus confusions, result from an overload of subplotting in the novel and an adaptation to film that extends the agony. Too many of the story's inducements seem strained; large and trifling particulars are less an assurance of convincing realities than they are story hindrances: Babe Levy (Dustin Hoffman) is in training for a marathon (Hoffman was nearly forty years old at casting and of neither body type nor running form to earn credible Olympic aspirations); Babe's brother, Doc Levy, is a (rogue) C.I.A. agent involved in a manufactured scheme with fugitive Nazis; and the Levy brothers' father had been a target of the McCarthy-era witch hunts.

The infamous dental scene actually exists in two parts (and two DVD chapters): "Dentistry — Is it Safe?" and "The Drill," parted by an insert chapter, "Apparent Rescue," not titled to sustain curiosity, let alone suspense.

Nazi Szell, surfacing in New York City, supposes that preparations are in the works to rob him of the plundered wealth long secreted in a bank, so Szell's painful dentistry on Babe's mouth is an attempt to "extract" cloak-and-dagger info.

Following Babe's re-abduction, a close-up on him composes a blurred, but certain, door opening behind him. The depth of field is slim so that Szell remains in soft focus until he fully gets to Babe, who is costumed still in the bathrobe and striped pajama bottoms he was wearing at the time of the first abduction and is once more secured to the chair in the soiled warehouse. Now in sharp focus, Szell's hand encouragingly pats Babe's shoulder. The camera tilts down and pulls back so that a large tray of dental instruments comes into view, with poor Babe in pajamas resembling a baby in a high chair. The camera continues back and to the right, eventually revealing a wide shot and Szell, professional as ever, washing well before his next procedure.

Throughout the scene's opening moments, Szell narrates the ruse played in the "Apparent Rescue": "The gun had blanks, the knife a retractable blade. Hardly original, but effective enough. I think you'll agree."

I think *you'll* agree that people in the audience would be incapable of sustaining life if, without clarification, the faked rescue befuddled them. It is a tribute to good actors everywhere that such dialogue gets delivered with credence.

The camera continues its move right, bringing it behind Babe, synchronized to Szell's arrival at the dentist's worktable; all the while, Szell is engaged in small (patronizing) talk, until he shares thoughts on diamond appraisals and the risks that may await him.

Szell plugs an electrical cord into a wall outlet, and although the tool is hidden by an open attaché case, we easily identify the fleeting whir of a drill.

THE *MARATHON MAN* MOMENT: 1:22:28–1:23:26

Babe stammers, "I don't know anything."

Szell calls out for one of his henchman, "Karl!"

Karl comes up behind Babe, who desperately tries to shield himself by bending forward, bracing his face in his lap.

He does not succeed. His mouth is opened and a rubber shield is placed across his lower teeth.

Szell dispassionately assures him, "Oh please, don't worry. I'm not going into that cavity. That nerve's already dying. A live freshly cut nerve is infinitely more sensitive. So I'll just drill into a healthy tooth until I reach the pulp... unless of course you can tell me that it's safe."

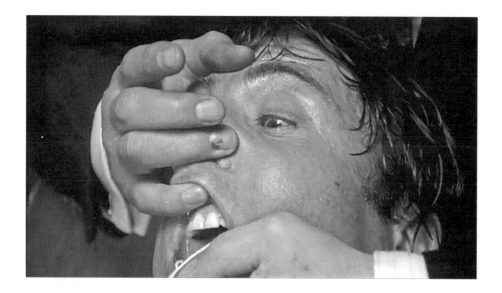

The small drill makes its way closer and closer to the camera till it is unrecognizably blurred. Its whine is unmistakable. The camera tilts and pans right (there is likely a dissolve across the blur) to rack-focus on a close-up of Szell's face, unperturbed and attentive. The camera then pans left into the bright, full light of a work lamp just as we hear Babe shriek.

Is it any wonder that word of mouth (as they say) about this scene filled movie houses? But, ironically, it is also true that many in the audience stepped out of the auditorium for a restroom or cigarette time-out, incapable of sitting for "The Drill."

MARIA FULL OF GRACE (2004)

"[This] superb independent film [tells] one of the emblematic migration stories of our time."
— David Denby, *New Yorker*, July 26, 2004

"The movie, which opens today in New York and Los Angeles, portrays Maria's story as a variation of the predicament that draws thousands of young Colombian women into the drug trade. Courted by a charming, motorcycle-riding recruiter she meets in a club, she is introduced to his ominously soothing boss, who lays out the rules and invites her to try out for the role of illicit courier. [The film] sustains a documentary authenticity that is as astonishing as it is offhand."
— Stephen Holden, *New York Times*, July 16, 2004

Seventeen-year-old Maria commutes daily to a rose plantation out-side Bogotá, Colombia, for labor-intensive work in the pruning and shipping of the beautiful and fragrant flower. The (mostly) female employees are uniformed in denim, large padded gloves, and tinted safety glasses as protection from the sharpness of shears and the nicks and stabs of thorns. The milieu is much like that of a correctional facility, which is especially apparent in the gathering for a lunchtime meal of bread and a piece of fruit.

An engaging irony is exposed when Maria undertakes a far more lucrative job requiring her conversion to a person-package, a "mule" to cart cocaine to America. Assumptions about illegal entry into the United States, and concerns about drug trafficking from Central and South America, establish an up-to-date backdrop to the story: No matter the viewer's penchant for prosecution and punishment, the pretty unfussiness of Maria's face easily wins us over. Her enticing juvenile eyes confront the viewer so that, though witness to foul deeds, we are inclined to keep silent and "pray" for Maria's success. Movies are especially memorable if sympathy and charity are awakened in the audience when story par-ticulars should educe neither. Maria glows with saintliness; forbidden behaviors are worthy of absolution — the film's title sways mercy.

Maria rehearses the fundamentals of her mission: She attempts to swallow large red grapes, eager to get the hang of restraining her gag reflex. She stands before a bathroom mirror — we are seeing her in reflection — her actions made clear by the attention in her eyes, and the plastic bag of grapes dropped into a small sink at the scene's outset. A small white wire basket of grooming lotions hangs on the wall to screen left.

Her efforts do not end so much in failure as in promoting audience concern. We do not see Maria successfully swallow a grape. She pokes the fruit far down her throat and hugs the wide tubelike muscle along the front of her neck. At the scene's conclusion, Maria choke-coughs up the grape, and exhaling, she gazes down to it in her hand and back into the mirror.

The next day she sits curbside with her suitcase, awaiting a ride with the motorcycle-riding recruiter. He arrives and with courtesy carries her suitcase to his bike and drives her to an open-fronted pharmacy shop. An illicit drug lab, secreted behind and above the open streetside shop of shelves displaying personal hygiene products, is accessed by a sliding wall of toothpaste.

THE *MARIA FULL OF GRACE* MOMENT: 0:39:44–0:42:33

Maria climbs a flight of stairs and directly enters a room busy with preparations. She takes note for herself (and us) of a man with scissors and a gloved right hand, clipping off fingers from a latex glove. Maria sits at a small table. A saucer and cup sit between her and a heavy metal-framed object that, we will soon learn, serves as vital equipment. The acoustic balance is near-echoing thin, with a periodically faint awareness of voices.

Maria watches the man — who makes no eye contact — fill the cut latex fingers with white cocaine powder. He concentrates fully on his task: He ties the open end of the latex package with a white string, and then presses the filled large-caliber-bulletlike capsule into a metal cylinder. He plunges this "cocaine bullet" with a pistonlike attachment on the heavy metal frame, and then pushes the capsule free. Finally he double-back folds the portion of the latex finger that extends beyond the filled portion, crafting a safety shield of dual thickness, and gently adds it to a bowl already holding quite a few tightly shaped capsules.

A man in a white lab coat, the same man who escorted Maria from the street pharmacy to her place at the table, brings her pills and water — to "slow your digestion." He then instructs, "Open your mouth; open," and as he sprays a bright red analgesic mist, intended to diminish the gag response, to the back of her throat, a calm, bearded old man, walking with the aid of a cane, passes behind her and sits alongside. This man was introduced to Maria in an earlier scene, a time when her "charming" boyfriend completed initial arrangements.

A bowl with latex-wrapped capsules of cocaine — giant suppositories to be launched at another end — is brought to the table, set alongside a bowl of clear, slightly viscous broth. The bearded man dips the first capsule into the liquid: "Here." Maria carefully takes hold with her fingers and places it into her mouth as she shifts her head back. With lips closed tight, Maria endeavors to relax the muscles of her throat, but a gentle whimper and a shift forward signifies an inability to swallow. She picks the capsule out from her mouth. Maria and the bearded man exchange a glance; she exhales, and shifting her head back again, she inserts the capsule farther into her throat. "Don't stick your fingers so far inside," the bearded man instructs, but Maria gag-coughs and pulls out the capsule.

The bearded man is too busy for delay. "If you can't do this, we'll stop right now." Maria quickly replies, "No, no. I know I can do it." She's allowed another try: "Let's see." Maria, in close-up, once again

shifts her head back and inserts the capsule. Her eyes scan the ceiling and we can watch the "play" of the muscles at the front of her throat. "Relax," the old man says — the back of his head in blur to the right of the screen — "Let it slide down." Maria shuts her eyes, and after a modest quiver, followed by an evident squinting-gulp, she overcomes her gag response and the capsule is down.

"Very good," acknowledges the old man, and he immediately dips another capsule into the soup.

The scene is crafted to end at this moment. A cut brings us Maria, standing with hands to her hips gradually pacing the room. Her ordeal is well under way, but she is taking a break from swallowing. "How many is it so far?" The answer: "Twenty-three."

On the table awaits thirty-nine more white capsules.

The audience easily suffers awareness of human gag reflex — an involuntary (ancestral) response to olfactory offenses and ingestion risks. It is believed that evolutionary tuning fashioned an anatomical configuration in the passageways of our esophagus and trachea that allowed for a larynx location enabling a vast assortment of sounds and, as a result, proficiency for spoken language — but it has also meant that we are a species carrying an increased danger of choking.

It is also disturbing that the grandfatherly bearded man, with cruel serenity, puts forward vengeful promises if the dope does not arrive at its destination.

CACHÉ (2005)

"[The film] begins, as many do, with an exterior establishing shot.... The camera, perfectly still, lingers for an unusually long time.... It turns out that this is not only the opening shot in a movie, but also part of a surveillance video.... [Director Michael] Haneke has deposited his audience at the Hitchcockian junction where voyeurism intersects with paranoia.... Variations on that enigmatic, implacable opening shot pop up again and again, intensifying the ambience of suspicion and multiplying the film's ironies and implications."

— A. O. Scott, *New York Times*, December 23, 2005

"In the opening minutes Anne and her husband, Georges, receive a videotape that suggests that their lives are being scrutinized by a spy. As the fear of being watched intensifies, so the secrets of Georges's past come to light.... The movie turns into a pitiless probing of France's colonialist hangover. Some people will find it horribly harsh, and a little prior knowledge of modern French history might be useful; on its own terms, though, the film, not least in the creepiness of its open ending, remains an efficient wrecker of nerves."

— Anthony Lane, *New Yorker*, January 9, 2006

The surreptitious camera, central to the plot, engenders a challenge to craft, requiring lucidity between camera as photographic instrument to filmmaking and camera as hidden spy; my friends and colleagues hold staggeringly varied outlooks on the images, their demands in storytelling, and their significance to premise.

The film disturbs in episodic substance and, eventually, in its moral tenacity: it asks of us an assumption of responsibility that idiom, adage, and law have long rejected. Its "pitiless probing of France's colonialist hangover" easily extends to Austria-Germany's noxious anti-Semitism — the director is Austrian — and to inequity and grievance everywhere.

A childhood, and childish, offense exacts profoundly extensive penalties, eternal from forebears through descendants: The story links Georges' unsettling surveillance videos and violent drawings to Majid, an Algerian whose parents worked on a provincial farm owned by Georges' family, and to events of October 17, 1961, when hundreds of Algerian protestors were killed by Paris policemen, ironically under the command of Maurice Papon, a former Nazi collaborator.

Georges confronts Majid at the man's cheerless apartment. The Algerian denies involvement with the harassing videos and drawings.

Later, following a near-paranoid entanglement concerning the police and Georges' "vanished" son, a telephone call interrupts work at a television station's digital postproduction facility, where Georges is employed. "What do you want now?"

The *Caché* Moment: 1:27:46–1:29:46

At the cut, Georges approaches the camera. He is in the hallway that leads to Majid's apartment. In medium shot he rings the buzzer. The wait at the door is nearly long enough to have Georges consider another ring when the door is unlocked and opened; the two men face each other across the width of the screen.

"What's going on?"

"Thanks for coming."

Majid backs out of the frame. "Come in."

Georges enters the apartment. A cut brings a master shot of the kitchen. It is over this shot that we hear — off-screen — the apartment door easily close. Georges follows Majid into the kitchen from a narrow foyer. "What's this all about?"

Majid closes the soft-yellow kitchen door. "Sit down."

Georges remains standing, "No," and turns toward Majid. "I won't. What do you want?"

"I truly had no idea about the tapes."

Georges shifts his hands outward, dropping them to the sides of his raincoat. "Is that all?"

"I called you because I wanted you to be present."

Majid fumbles to reach into his pants pocket. His untucked shirt gets in the way, but he pulls-out and opens a barber's style shaving razor. Georges takes a small though hasty step back. Majid, with the razor in his right hand, reaches across to the left side of his own neck and draws the blade forward. Breath and blood detonate, hitting high on door and wall. Majid crumples at once.

Georges' memory from age six, long hidden and personally inconsequential, has unexpectedly come due, and he is fixed in place. When he takes slow steps to frame right, Majid's blood is visible, seeping along the kitchen floor. For a few moments Georges leaves the frame entirely, his shadow alone along the edge of the screen.

The briefest moment before the self-killing ceded fears of Georges' security and emphasized the event's resolute shame; so brutal a suicide, attended by a foe, is conclusive and enduring psychological horror.

Georges re-enters the frame with restrained persistent chokes.

As witness, in but a single composition, the audience is the surveillance camera's eye. At scene's end, Georges — spiritually incarcerated — remains in Majid's kitchen.

*Strip the phony tinsel off Hollywood and
you'll find the real tinsel underneath.*

— Oscar Levant

SPECTACLE

In joyful benefit to my dozen cousins, and near carefree charity to our moms, till the dads arrived every Friday night via the Long Island Railroad and left early Monday morning, back to Manhattan and a new week of work, our Aunt Helen was the self-styled June-to-Labor Day camp counselor. She organized homespun games tallied with silver and gold stars on an oversized illustration board with all our names posted. All-purpose good deeds, or a helping hand in the community kitchen, added more stars and the possibility of a toy reward or an ice-cream sundae at a corner parlor, where the bus from the railroad station let the dads off.

We spent so many summertime evenings ambling the boardwalk — staying, as rules had it, within sight of Aunt Helen — from Long Beach's west-end bungalows eastward past commanding hotels to the amusement arcades, peewee Ferris wheel, and cotton candy counter. It seems even now an unexpected setting for a movie theater, but my aunt was sure: right beyond the miniature golf course, *King Kong* was playing inside the Jackson Hotel.

On a night Aunt Helen had set up marshmallow roasting at a beach bonfire — helping gather driftwood could earn a star — she reported that *King Kong* was coming to Long Beach; and we were captivated when she told about seeing the movie in her Brooklyn neighborhood during the Great Depression. She divulged a few details directly, others by hint, but mostly she'd say, "I don't want to tell you because it will ruin the movie." And so, as is the case in childhood, the anticipation made little fanatics of us all, raring to get going every second of the two (or three) days between news about Kong's arrival and heading down the boardwalk.

The approach to the Jackson lifted my misgivings: There, on both sides of the hotel's entranceway, were *King Kong* posters!

The word "awesome," a late twentieth-century exclamation for just about everything, doesn't ring a memory bell from the early half of the

1950s — "incredible," "terrific," and "wow" do — but when my aunt handed out the tickets one at a time, and I in turn presented mine to enter the Jackson lobby, all at once hearing the brassy calamity score and biplane motors with machine guns snarling through a red leather-padded puffy door, I was awestruck. A small diamond-shaped window was sited barely within tiptoe viewing, and so I lengthened to peek into the auditorium in time to catch the last moments of the beast atop the Empire State Building, fending off the army air squadron, until my cousin Arthur pointed me out, and Aunt Helen said, "Richard, be patient for the next showing."

At last the puffy red door opened, and the moviegoers crowded out of the theater and onto the boardwalk. But before the auditorium emptied enough for us to rush in and get the best seats, the lobby lights dimmed, then flickered and quit — an electrical mess-up did us in, and there was no next showing.

My aunt was first in line to get our money back, and all the gloomy way west, we stuck to the rules, keeping in sight of her.

It would be many years before I finally got to see the rest of *King Kong*. I went by myself. Yet the movie's moment I remember most is the one I viewed through the diamond-shaped glass at the Jackson Hotel — that none of my cousins got to see.

KING KONG (1933)

"The ultimate monster movie and one of the grandest and most beloved adventure films ever made, *King Kong* has given us one of the most enduring icons of American popular culture.... At the height of the Great Depression, [it] grossed $1,761,000 and by itself saved the studio from bankruptcy. In 1938, the studio decided to re-release its classic, but took several steps to tone it down. The film had been made before... the Production Code began to be vigorously enforced.... Cut were the scenes of Kong chewing and crushing human beings. Gone was the scene in which a curious Kong strips Fay Wray of her clothing."

— *movies.tvguide.com*

"At both the Radio City Music Hall and the RKO Roxy, which have a combined seating capacity of 10,000, the main attraction now is a fantastic film.... When the enormous ape is brought to this city, the excitement

reaches its highest pitch. Imagine a fifty-foot beast with a girl in one paw climbing up the outside of the Empire State Building."
— Mordaunt Hall, *New York Times*, March 3, 1933

"[The film] is so excessive, so grotesque and absurd, that it makes even the events of the day seem temperate and commonplace.... Somewhat like a nightmare one might have dozing away by chance in the shadows of the Natural History Museum, the ridiculous film presents a mammoth ape of prehistoric build inhabiting an unchartered island somewhere west of Sumatra. In the course of the story the ape is captured and brought to New York, and eventually we have the spectacle of the thing perched on top of the Empire State Building, the facade of which he has had no difficulty in climbing."
— John C. Mosher, *New Yorker*, March 11, 1933

"'It was not the guns that got him,' says one of the characters at the end, after Kong has been brought to ground by a whole squadron of battle planes. 'It was Beauty killed the Beast.' By having Beauty in the person of Miss Wray lure the great monster to his destruction, the scenario writers sought to unite two rather widely separated traditions of the popular cinema — that of the thriller and that of the sentimental romance. The only difficulty was that they failed to realize that such a union was possible only by straining our powers of credulity and perhaps also one or two fundamental laws of nature. For if the love that Kong felt for the heroine was sacred, it suggests a weakness that hardly fits in with his other actions; and if it was, after all, merely profane, it proposes problems to the imagination that are not the less real for being crude."
— William Troy, *Nation*, March 22, 1933

I am particularly struck by Troy's probing of the blend of movie genres and cross-species erotica, providing a tone of civility while encouraging "monstrous" imaginings. According to the notes on the back of my DVD, when director Merian C. Cooper approached a Hollywood mogul for financial backing, the studio chief asked, "You know what a 50-foot gorilla would see in a 5-foot girl?" And he quickly answered his own question: "His breakfast!" The relationship of beauty and the beast founded on digestion? Wouldn't that have hampered the scenario writers? With a mealtime proposal offered by a Hollywood mogul, I'd have guessed they'd "do lunch." But if, as reported by the *TV Guide* movie database, Kong did (in a deleted scene) remove Fay Wray's clothing, then Troy was on to something!

In fact, in 1931, a "couple of New York-based sharpies" got hold of grainy "African documentary footage shot in 1914," spliced it together with a variety of provocative topless and exotic scenes, combined with a "chap in a rented gorilla suit" and released *Ingagi* (Congo Pictures/ RKO). The confident orange, black, green, and white movie poster reveals a gorilla — eyes and maw gaudily intoxicated — holding a tilting bare-breasted native woman; the gorilla's right hand cups the woman's right breast. The text: "Wild Women – Gorillas – Unbelievable! *INGAGI* The Most Sensational Picture Ever Filmed!" I could find no review of *Ingagi* in the *New Yorker*.

During World War I, a gorilla (with eyes bulged and mouth drooling) carrying off a bare-breasted beauty (one hand hiding her eyes) appeared in a propaganda poster — "Destroy This Mad Brute" — encouraging enlistment in the U.S. Army. The gorilla embodied German militarism.

It is alleged that the scene of Kong's battle with the elevated train was a last-minute addition to extend the film past a first cut that was thirteen reels long: Merian C. Cooper was superstitious.

You will also see Cooper and his codirector and coproducer, Ernest B. Schoedsack, in the Empire State Building scene. They are the gesturing flyers in one of the biplanes and appear in four cuts at 1:38:37, 1:38:56, 1:39:17, and 1:41:33.

A vital reference to credible scale is realized with a number of inventively composed master shots constructed from models, paintings, and merged elements: Four biplanes take off from an airfield. The first of the two shots holds a panoramic view of Manhattan as a backdrop; an extreme long shot of the Empire State Building, precisely centered in the frame, promptly spots Kong ascending the edge of the right side; the four biplanes fly high in an unadorned sky; a medium shot has the biplanes flying parallel to (and just above) the camera, followed by a return to the Empire State Building, where we see Kong reach the very top as the planes approach from screen right.

The score is reminiscent of the serial shorts of the day, the tension equivalent. We might value the military flyer's dedication to duty while, at this moment, compassion for the "beast" is keenly in place; and we dread unintended damage to Ann (Fay Wray) by Kong or biplanes. So it is not inconsequential that the beast sets her aside.

THE *KING KONG* MOMENT: 01:39:29–01:39:57

A single plane flies straight up and loops upside down to the right. In an almost elegant lounge, on the edge along the base of the building's domed top, in something more negligee-like than evening gown, is Fay Wray, looking up at the high-flying maneuvers. A second plane dives from the squadron formation of three to strike Kong as he straddles the spikelike tower of the building's observation dome. The image of King Kong is made all the more impressive with a backdrop of an airborne look across Manhattan: the Chrysler Building — then the second tallest (after the Empire State Building) in the world — to screen right, and beyond a view of the Queensboro Bridge (Fifty-Ninth Street Bridge), Roosevelt Island, and the East River. At the time, the slim strip of land below the bridge was Welfare Island (1921–1973) and the location of a smallpox hospital.

The plane attacks and zooms upward as Kong swats at it, his angry face dropping below the frame as the plane's POV displays a full light-gray frame into which the back of the plane enters and banks to the right. The last two planes dive in a shrill roar, and we see the dual-flyer cockpit with a fuselage-mounted machine gun. Then, for me, the most astonishing image of all: We soar toward Kong as if in the trailing

fighter — tight in the wake of the observable gun-blasting plane just ahead. Kong glowers and counters with a swipe at us both — and at this precise moment, cousin Arthur snitched!

ALEXANDER NEVSKY (1938)

"Sergei Eisenstein's classic tale of 13th-century Russia is as magnificent today as it must have been in 1938.... This epic concerns the trying period when Russia was invaded by Teutonic knights on one front and Tartars on the other; the motherland is plundered, the moody, volatile Prince Nevsky forms his army (an undertaking that consumes half the film), then wins a decisive battle at frozen Lake Peipus.... [The director] had the Russian army at his disposal, and the battle scenes, populated with thousands of men, are overwhelming. [The galloping Teutonic knights] wear terrifying helmets fashioned after gargoyles and ogres.... [Sergei] Prokofiev's vigorous score has become a concert piece in its own right."

— *movies.tvguide.com*

After more than six years of unproductivity, not all of it voluntary, Sergei Eisenstein, the D. W. Griffith of the Russian screen, has returned to party favor and to public honors with this rough-hewn monument to national heroism, which had its New World unveiling at the Cameo last night.... It is the picture which prompted Josef Stalin to slap its maker on the back and exclaim, 'Sergei, you are a true Bolshevik.' And, it is a picture, moreover, which sets up this morning an unusual problem in reviewing.

For Eisenstein's work can no more withstand the ordinary critical scrutiny, a judgment based on the refinement and subtlety of its execution than, say, the hydraulic sculpture and rock blasting that Gutzon Borglum is dashing off on Mount Rushmore. Eisenstein is sublimely indifferent to detail, whether narrative or pictorial.... His concern, obvious from the start, is only with the broad outline of his film, its most general narrative and scenic contours. His picture... is primarily a picture of a battle and it must stand, or fall, solely upon Eisenstein's generalship in marshaling his martial array.... It is a stunning battle, this reenactment of his of the beautiful butchery that occurred one Winter's day in 1242.... It is impossible not to marvel at his stylistic insistence that all people walk along a skyline, and not to wish, in the same breath, that more directors had his talent for doing great things so well and little things so badly."

— Frank S. Nugent, *New York Times*, March 23, 1939

The thirteenth-century setting of foreign invasion and patriotic heroism was intended by the director as a cautionary tale to Nazi Germany — the menace of Hitler to 1938 Europe and mother Russia — and a proclamation of triumphant assurance to the Soviet people. Eisenstein characterized this work, his first sound film, as "vertical montage": the communication and correlation of "the image of the orchestral score with the montage structure of the silent film."

Unlike the director's earlier films, *Strike*, *The Battleship Potemkin*, and *October*, this story more willingly considered the valor of the individual rather than (purely) collective achievements. Eisenstein also employed a more conservative narrative, allowing for a subplot of a rivalry between two soldiers for the hand of a young woman who stands, as do her suitors, with the valiant Russians gathered on the frozen lake.

The film designates its own selection: "The Battle on Ice" scene. And yet, from my original viewing at the Thalia (Ninety-Fifth Street on the Upper West Side of Manhattan, closed in 1987 and currently going through refurbishment as Symphony Space), sometime between 1960 and 1961, the joining in battle endured less memorably than did the ("vertical montage") moments of expectation.

THE *ALEXANDER NEVSKY* MOMENT: 0:57:46–0:59:42

April 5, 1242, Lake Chudskoye: The film frame is divided into two very unequal parts. In an aspect ratio of 1.33:1 (a measurement of the horizontal to vertical "square" of early movie frames), the sky extravagantly entertains 95%, while the frosty snow cover holds a horizon of 5%, with a line of Teutonic knights, an early Germanic clan, nearly across its entire width. The initial rhythmic throb of composer Sergei Prokofiev's score takes on a low snarling horn as the far-off knights advance. This shot holds the screen for more than half a minute.

A cut now devises a frame in three parts. The sky still manages its great dominance over the snow-covered ground, with the knights visible on the horizon, but on the right side of the frame, with a softness that only comes about through thousands of years of weather wear or if carpenter constructed, a colossal boulder advances to about one-half of the frame height and one-third of its width. Atop it stand five men, three holding long staffs, and quite a few men can be seen at its base, both front and back. Many more staffs are in evidence.

Another cut displays a frame much like the first — very high sky with Teutonic knights at the horizon — but this time with a gathering of men with staffs in the left frame foreground. The next cut duplicates the first but for an ever-so-miniscule increase in the size of the knights

as they gallop toward the foreground and Prince Nevsky's peasant army. Eisenstein is taking his (extended) time to bring the armies into combat: The anticipation of confrontation drives the pacing to, and with, Prokofiev's grand score.

Next comes the first image of the front defensive line of the Russians, a line that runs the full width of the frame. The foreground shows foot soldiers at the left but a trifle lower in the frame than the diminishing scale of men to the right. Now banners and shields enhance the many vertical staffs.

The overwhelming sky is continued across a series of cuts of the awaiting Russians — calm in contrast to the fast-moving knights; and, also in contrast, the gallant Russian faces are fully visible under their helmets, while the faces of the Teutons are concealed by monstrous armored masks.

An intense horn signals several cuts of the galloping knights moving across screen right to left, in ever closer compositions. The last of these is a set piece on a live stage, a rendition of a fast-moving mounted army portrayed with banners sliding across the background, while helmeted knights, fastened in place, shift symmetrically up and down, as when riding the gear-shaft ponies of a carousel — magical allusions facilitated by the "collective" skills of Prokofiev and Eisenstein.

Anticipation shows on the faces of the Russian soldiers. As the one-minute mark in the Teutons' advance is approached, "The Germans" is announced.

Prince Nevsky, his portrait in profile, displays resolve and vigor.

In all there are four minutes of Eisenstein's spectacular images united in time with Prokofiev's majestic music — and then the Germans crash the Russian line.

The Thalia's undersized hall positioned the screen barely inches above the floor. This was a just-right fit for the small containerlike screening room: the auditorium perceptibly conveyed the 1938 aspect ratio in a cube.

PATHS OF GLORY (1957)

"Stanley Kubrick's first great film established the epic style that has served him so well since. The film was banned in France [for] eighteen years because of its anti-militarist stance."
— *movies.tvguide.com*

"This is a story — based on an actual occurrence, by the way — that reflects not alone on France's honor but also on the whole concept of military authority. [This] unembroidered, documentary-like account opened at the Victoria yesterday. Also, merely as a footnote — what a picture to open on Christmas Day!"
— Bosley Crowther, *New York Times*, December 26, 1957

> "Humphrey Cobb's famous novel of 1935 has finally been adapted to the screen, putting an end to a good deal of nervous nail-biting on the part of American moviemakers who have been circling and sniffing at the property for two decades. Cobb's intention was to demonstrate not simply that war is hell, but also that it is a gigantic swindle — a proposition that, considering the tenor of the times, naturally gave pause to men who had no desire to upset any popular applecarts."
>
> — John McCarten, *New Yorker*, January 4, 1958

McCarten's review title, "The Old Army Game," cynically indicts the agents of the "gigantic swindle" — political and martial old men — who eternally manage the hell of war as a righteous and gallant calling. Are no lessons learned and realized from the many profound antiwar verdicts found in film and literature? Perhaps, as Woody Allen expressed, "No matter how cynical you get, you can't keep up."

Director Stanley Kubrick was not yet thirty years of age when he asked Kirk Douglas to star in this film; and Douglas — intuitive about "upsetting any applecarts" — responded, "Stanley, I don't think this picture will ever make a nickel, but we have to make it."

The "actual [World War I] occurrence" on which the film is based was similarly plotted twenty-three years later in director Bruce Beresford's *Breaker Morant*, based on an "actual occurrence" of the Boer War. There are, of course, many others from the past, and sadly, we can all be certain, still more to follow.

I went to see Kubrick's film when I was fifteen years old. As a Stanislavsky-trained actor attempts to draw on connections to his character's circumstances by a concentrated exploration into his own, often intimate, "sense memories," my recall of this movie is so meticulously corporeal that memories, I suspect, are stored neither singly nor in a solitary region of the brain but transverse vicinities of explicitness while by-chance bursts tinker with one region, then two, then others en route to conscious conversion.

Three years after my father moved us to year-round residence in our Nassau County summertime town, I went alone to the Kubrick film on a sunny and cold afternoon, bundled in the popular mid-1950s large box-pocketed woolen duffle coat, effectively latched with horn-long shoots that slipped into loops of rope — a high and deep hood attached at the back — walking west along out-of-season streets on Long Beach's West Broadway to Laurelton Boulevard, then north from Pine Street to Beech then Olive, Walnut and Park Avenue, to the Laurel Theatre. There was not a single other moviegoer at the ticket window, and the family-size box of Raisinettes bought at the patron-less concession counter attended me to the best seat in the empty auditorium.

French General Mireau has ordered Colonel Dax (Kirk Douglas) to capture the German position known as the Ant Hill. The plan of attack is to begin with an artillery barrage at 0515. At 0530 the First Battalion is to move out. At zero minus two minutes, General Mireau — a frequent and too loud chortler — shares his flask of cognac with his staff: "To France."

Wearing a fresh and tailored tunic, Dax steps along the twisting dugout of the front line, passing shabby and drained soldiers via an absolutely wondrous tracking shot, which moves backward in advance of Dax and is intercut with a forward-moving tracking shot that is his POV, conducted with airy squeals and blasts of ammo across the field.

My latest screenings — alone and with students — convince me that the expectation of battle, accessible in the trench-tracking intercuts, will supply another and likely more significant memorable moment in much the same way as does the anticipation before Eisenstein's "The Battle on Ice."

Two seconds before the infantry offensive is to start, Dax scurries up a ladder, and no sooner out of the trench, he fiercely blows whistle signals that launch the battalion.

THE *PATHS OF GLORY* MOMENT: 0:28:57–0:31:56

The assault to take the Ant Hill is first covered in an overhead panorama of the field, accompanied by multiple blasts of the colonel's whistle and white puffs of shell smoke. Dax, armed with whistle and pistol, waves his men forward. A sport's-stadium-like roar from the advancing army nearly overwhelms all other combat sounds.

To provide a low profile to enemy fire, Dax crouches sporadically as the camera tracks him left across the screen, past wire and gouged-earth obstacles. At times the lens' depth of field is so narrow that charging soldiers in the foreground are a blur, displaying images of photojournalistic value: There is little visible sky, and what there is of it is vacant; the zoom and (simultaneous) tracking grant a compelling feel of frenzied and frightful participation that commits itself to memory.

I now believe the heightened perceptions of more than a half century ago have been broadened by the movie's affecting wallop — the grunge of battlefield trenches presented in a gray temper of such sopping dreariness — that my mind has archived the arousing essence with its own imposing truth: It is one thing to recall no other patron at the ticket window or purchasing snacks at the lobby concession, but my memory also insists that there was no one else in attendance, and neither a vehicle nor pedestrian en route to or from the theater. I don't think this could be true, but I do believe that I'd pass a lie-detector test if I so testified. Kubrick's work has convincingly altered the memory of all that came to light that winter day.

I am still (more or less) certain that the solemn — if not grave — privileged screening obliged me to put the jumbo box of candy into my pocket till the movie had ended and I was on my way home, desperate for sweet relief.

APOCALYPSE NOW (1979)

"Despite its flaws, one of the most complex and unforgettable war movies ever made."
— *movies.tvguide.com*

"Francis Coppola's [film] lives up to its grand title, disclosing not only the various faces of war, but also the contradictions between excitement and boredom, terror and pity, brutality and beauty. When it [evokes] the look and feelings of the Vietnam War, dealing in sense impressions for which no explanations are adequate or necessary, [the film] is a stunning work... though it wants to be something more than a kind of cinematic tone poem. Mr. Coppola himself describes it as 'operatic.' Ultimately, [it] is neither a tone poem nor an opera. It's an adventure yarn with delusions of grandeur, a movie that ends — in the all-too-familiar words of the poet Mr. Coppola drags in by the boot straps — not with a bang, but a whimper. Vittorio Storaro is responsible for the extraordinary camerawork that almost, but not quite, saves [the film] from its profoundly anticlimactic intellectual muddle."
— Vincent Canby, *New York Times*, August 15, 1979

"For better or for worse, the movie confirms the idea that a work of art consists of local particulars. To use somebody else's work of art as a skeleton, you first have to turn it into a skeleton. Where [the movie] is least successful (the last half hour), it seems to have been made by people who have read Conrad with their teeth. Where it is amazingly successful (the first two hours), it takes least from Conrad — or, rather, it takes subtly and delicately, for form and inspiration."
— Veronica Geng, *New Yorker*, September 3, 1979

Director Francis Ford Coppola dropped his middle name for the release of his adaptation of Joseph Conrad's *Heart of Darkness*. The evaluation in hindsight from the *TV Guide* movie database "recommends" the movie for the Inspired or Epoch categories in genre alone; Coppola's fixing on the Vietnam War — and its substantial bearing on the politics and principles of a drawn-out era — could promote such placements, but the "flaws," "delusions of grandeur," and "intellectual muddle" accentuate the "operatic" and Spectacle. For me, however, the movie is so laboriously scene driven — the whole barely equals the sum of its parts — that I am choosing a moment that exhibits a premise specific to Vietnam, a tip taken from the *New Yorker* reviewer:

with appreciated insight, Geng argues that the greater influence on the director was Michael Herr's book *Dispatches* and Coppola's authorship of the Captain Benjamin Willard (Martin Sheen) narration, "the weary, laconic why-am-I-even-bothering-to-tell-you language of the pulp private eye."

From the outset — multiple exposures of fire and helicopters and ceiling fan whirs; an upside-down sweat-faced Willard; window blinds; and flippant voiceover — it is that!

Willard has been assigned to proceed down the coast in a U.S. Navy PBR (a plastic patrol boat) into the Nung River to Nu Mung Ba to locate the erratically insane Special Forces Colonel Walter E. Kurtz, who, with his Montagnard army, has betrayed all semblance of legitimate command. Willard is to terminate the colonel.

The captain's narration introduces the boat's crew via arduous exposition: "The crew were mostly just kids... Rock 'n' Rollers with one foot in their graves." Mr. Clean, an African American seventeen-year-old is tagged as coming from "some South Bronx shit hole."

Clean is listening to an army broadcast on his transistor radio. The show's host announces a request from the mayor of Saigon that all GIs living off base hang their laundry not on window sills, but indoors, to keep Saigon looking beautiful.

THE *APOCALYPSE NOW* MOMENT: 0:23:08–0:24:14

As Willard reviews the Colonel Kurtz dossier, the radio resounds with the Rolling Stones' "I Can't Get No Satisfaction." Clean, with dog tags and cross dangling on his youthfully slim bare chest, grooves to the music, the transistor, with two feet of telescoping antenna, held tightly in his hand, his head protected from the sun and the enemy by a woolen Army beret.

A close-up of Willard directs the camera into a pan right as he swaps notice from Clean to the wake of the patrol boat and Lance, a surfer from South Los Angeles, now waterskiing off the stern.

The music blasts the pristine waterway as Chef, the machinist from New Orleans, hollers, "Hang on, Lance!"

A group of Vietnamese civilians — women and children — hurry back from waterside chores. Lance skis past with an arm-up salute.

Chef joins in the sing-a-long, and Clean struts his stuff across available deck. Willard goes back to studying Kurtz.

With a shout, "Look out, Lance," the patrol boat and the L.A. surfer bounce and hot-rod past two Vietnamese men in a primitive log catamaran, bicycles standing between them. Lance yelps a cowboy, "Yahoooo" and "Sayonara!" The Vietnamese men are toppled into the water.

Here is Spectacle, as in "make a spectacle, or fool, of yourself," and in a grand, globally boorish, ethnocentric manner.

RAN (1985)

"At age 75, Akira Kurosawa,... created one more magnificent work that will surely stand the test of time.... [He] turned to Shakespeare for inspiration — as he had in *Throne of Blood* nearly 30 years before — and [filmed] a Japanese adaptation of "King Lear."... [The film] is a visually stunning epic, containing some of the most beautiful, colorful, breathtaking imagery ever committed to celluloid... a true cinematic masterwork of sight, sound, intelligence and — most important — passion."

— *movies.tvguide.com*

"It would be difficult to imagine a more appropriate way to open the 23d New York Film Festival than with... Akira Kurosawa's *Ran (Chaos)*, a film of such grandeur that brings to mind Griffith's 'Birth of a Nation, Napoléon Vu par Abel Gance,' and Eisenstein's 'Ivan the Terrible.' [The film is] a visual masterwork, whose manners, which sometimes look old fashioned, recall virtually the entire history of epic cinema. Here is a film by a man whose art now stands outside time and fashion."

— Vincent Canby, *New York Times*, September 27, 1985

Kurosawa has said that *Ran* was inspired by a sixteenth-century Japanese warlord, not Shakespeare's *King Lear*, though the royal settings, the warlord's three offspring, and the family treacheries did "bring" Lear to Kurosawa. But this work is "epic" and a "cinematic masterwork" for it is *not* determined by dialogue or lexicon.

Hidetora Ichimonji, the seventy-year-old warlord and leader of the Ichimonji clan, has determined to yield his "empire" to his three sons, who must swear loyalty to him and each other. His desire to stand down after a half century of war and endow his conquered prosperity to Taro, Jiro, and Saburo directly ignites conflict.

Saburo, the youngest son, defies his father: "What kind of world do we live in? One barren of loyalty and feeling. You spilled an ocean of blood. You showed no mercy, no pity. We too are children of this age, weaned of strife and chaos. We are your sons, yet you count on our fidelity." The implications of Saburo's stance come to pass.

Hidetora awakens (from rest and illusion) to Taro's and Jiro's vast integrated attack upon their father. With the gruesome death of a trusted soldier, all noise of battle is set aside. For nearly six minutes, utter magnificence fulfills cinema's promise. Here is absolute evidence of Kurosawa's genius.

THE *RAN* MOMENT: 1:01:24–1:07:04

"[The director] has said of his epic spectacle that it is 'human deeds as viewed from heaven.' [Its] fiercest battles are serene, as if preordained. In a massacre at a fortress on the slopes of Mt. Fuji, where Hidetora sees his retinue and concubines butchered by his own sons' troops, Kurosawa cuts off the noise of the flaming arrows and the cries of the warriors and their victims; the carnage is a horror show, an elegiac ballet with no sound but Toru Takemitsu's harshly poignant music."

— Pauline Kael, *New Yorker*, January 13, 1986

The "natural" sounds of the setting resume; a gun blast tears into the mounted Taro. Treachery plays out. The eldest son is assassinated by Jiro's advisers.

Dare to be naïve.
— *Buckminster Fuller*

SENSUAL

Growing up in a ground-floor apartment in lower Manhattan evokes memories of surroundings so excessively utilitarian — there's no disowning marked sensations, but they were oddly physical while sensually deficient — that aesthetics only come to mind in dozens of my bright childhood crayon drawings; or in the Mediterranean-looking man who always appeared in good spirits over and over again on my bedroom wallpaper, along with two children (a boy and a girl and their terrier) who were pointing up to balloons held by curled strings in the man's hand; or in the likable little glassware for juice or milk that my mother habitually purchased on Essex or Orchard Streets. I bring up aesthetics because in early adolescence — and I was late to it — I found that visual artistry and attendant form granted a short distance to the sensual.

This was before I discovered Brigitte Bardot.

Oh! In pre-pre-adolescence, I was "exposed" to the famous Marilyn Monroe calendar. It hung on the wall at Harry's barber shop, no matter what year it was. At age four, when Harry first trimmed my hair, I did not know the model by name, but her pink luminous skin against the Chinese red drapery, posed in the company of Harry's customers, did instigate new thoughts on gender: I could detect a confused discomfort.

I recall everything else as practical: our kitchen table and matching chairs were capped in oilcloth of a rust-hued faux-marble swirl, and in every room the wood floors were sheltered under linoleum. The furnishings were a match in miscellany that my mother cleansed and polished with compulsive duty; she kept everything spot free.

She washed the family clothing by hand and ran it out to dry on a rope that my father fastened to the fire escape off their bedroom window, over a back alley and then to a sharply sloped utility pole, a distance of some forty feet. And there was many an afternoon that my father scaled the fire-escape ladder and dropped into the alley to

recover fallen laundry. Later my mother found out that she was permitted to use the brand-new coin-operated washing machines and dryers
in the basement of the housing projects across the street.

My mother not once sat to a meal in our kitchen; she nibbled as she
cooked for others, and noshed during the day on Limburger cheese. Its
stench could not be contained in the refrigerator, so she took a chunk
of farmer cheese — a benignly gentle milk curd product — from its
narrow dovetailed box and filled the box with the Limburger, keeping
it on the outside sill of a small kitchen window that faced a six-story
airshaft and a good flock of city pigeons that were somehow dispirited
from stealing the foodstuff — either the wood of the box or the dread
of the odor sheltered the Limburger. My mealtime chair sat at that
window, and the unpleasantness of that cheese (behind the pane) just
over my right shoulder jogs memories inside my nose. It must be true
that cells akin to those in the brain reside within our nostrils.

And so, for the most part, the dwelling of my early years fit flawlessly with the worse-for-wear Windsor movie house, its disheveled
candy counter man, and the obese matron with a flashlight and a huff.
Sergei Eisenstein's theory of juxtaposition was apparent to me before
the house lights at a Loews ever dimmed: it was a bravura happening!

A box office lady would greet us in a burgundy fitted jacket, a
reminder of the WWII Eisenhower jacket that self-confidently dressed
General Dwight David Eisenhower, who in 1953 became president of
the United States. The refreshment concession staff wore correspond-
ing costumes, and I suspect, though it was a time before such schemes,
that candy fragrances and a warming bouquet of butter and popcorn
were synthesized and atomized to bring delight and sales.

I remember an early walk onto (and a bit into) the abundant
lobby carpet, a severe contrast to linoleum or the stringy bath mat
that wrapped the edge of our tub and soothed wet feet on an otherwise chilled floor. Theater elegance was ordered with red velvet ropes
joined at gleaming brass fasteners; and the entryway glowed beneath
chandeliers as refined as they were high — so high that I could not
figure how anyone was going to change a spent bulb.

For less than a dollar, the working class (and those poorer), from one of the most densely populated neighborhoods in the world, could escape to the movies.

James Baldwin's lyrical recollection of attending his first movie made me mull over whims about illuminations and reflective surfaces — the sea, the glass-beaded movie screen. Even lacking the celluloid-snaking spools of a projector, *light*, I thought, is the mechanism of moviegoing sensuality. It is as a heavenly glow that ceaselessly shines in ever-widening arms that might marry the world.

HIROSHIMA MON AMOUR (1959)

"After spending 10 years making documentary shorts which were distinguished by their boldly experimental editing, [director] Alain Resnais made [this] extraordinary [film], which was originally intended to be a documentary about the reconstruction of Hiroshima, but evolved into being his first feature, [and which] remains one of the greatest and most auspicious feature-film debuts in [cinema history]."
— *movies.tvguide.com*

"[This] delicately wrought drama, which had its premiere at the Fine Arts Theatre yesterday, is a complex yet compelling tour de force — as a patent plea for peace and the abolition of atomic warfare, as a poetic invocation of love lost and momentarily found, as a curiously intricate but intriguing montage of thinking."
— A. H. Weiler, *New York Times*, May 17, 1961

"With [this, his first feature-film,] Alain Resnais, a thirty-seven year old Frenchman, hitherto unheralded, emerges as one of the best movie-makers of our time.... The story [is] of a brief, sad, hopeless love affair that is kindled between a Japanese architect and a French actress while she is on location in Hiroshima. This might sound like a twist on dear old 'Madame Butterfly,' but it is nothing of the sort, since M. Resnais [is] seeking to project a good many problems more intricate than those involved in miscegenation. What we have here is a kind of tract for our atomic times, but never once in the course of making a case against the lunacies of the era does M. Resnais bog his drama down in preachments."
— John McCarten, *New Yorker*, May 28, 1960

"The reaction that I remember was a very considerable elation and excitement, and there were parties. It would make a tremendously

interesting contrast, what was going on in Los Alamos at the same time as what was going on in Hiroshima. I was drinking and drunk, sitting on the bonnet of a Jeep playing drums, with excitement all over Los Alamos at the same time people were dying and struggling in Hiroshima."
— Physicist Richard Feynman, Reflections on August 6, 1945, BBC interview, 1981

A wondrous promise, inherent in a "boldly experimental" creative endeavor, has been kept: An intended movie about the reconstruction of Hiroshima, by an experienced documentary director, was *transmuted* — a physics term for the transformation of the atom of one chemical element into the atom of another through nuclear bombardment — into a first feature, celebrated as a "tour de force." Did the film form fully change? Is Alain Resnais' first feature-*length* film *only* in narrative?

McCarten's review gives ample account of the director's achievement and of the film's premise and scenario. Yet, the essentials of a love affair scarcely speak to the movie's genre or atmosphere. Weiler — so soon after viewing — was surely seeking access to "a curiously intricate but intriguing montage of thinking."

One would neither suspect nor suppose that a movie centered on the bomb-abolished city of Hiroshima could caress sensuality.

The contrasts that director Alain Resnais incorporates — sexual, tactile, and aural in a dream world and a hell, presented as documentary or narrative, as poetry or prose, as radio or literature, equally scored in music Eastern and Western, modern and primitive — are simultaneously perilous and soothing.

The *Hiroshima Mon Amour* Moment: 0:02:12–0:03:36

A very simple and sorrowful piano brings wrapped arms — a torso clasped. Is this an embrace of self, or an enfolding of two bodies, or more? Sand (or is it dust?) settles on bodies. An almost discordant note precedes a dissolve and piano strike, and the bodies are now under a flow of glistening particles; arms and hands seem to swarm over themselves and each other. Dampness appears, a nearly repulsive texture to the embracing, before another dissolve displays tempting skin. Clean and holding bodies, now accompanied by the sadness of a wind instrument, dissolve into a composition that is easily referenced in the

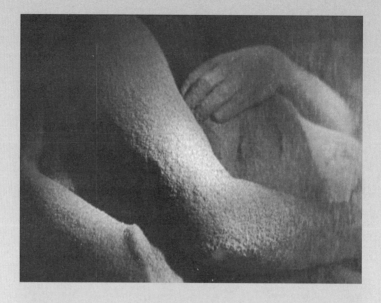

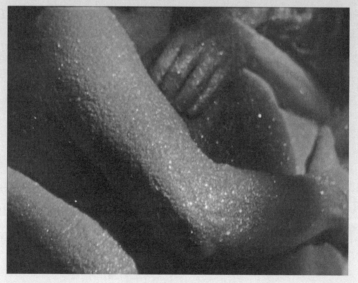

frame. It is a man; perspiration gleams on an arm that is inserted as support for a woman beneath him. The man's arm almost disappears into the blur of the distant frame as it folds into the background, cupping the woman's shoulder. Sweat coats the woman's arm as well. A dissolve again, and the frame fills with the man's back, the woman — hidden beneath him — is revealed in hands alone. They clutch the man's shoulders; the fingers of her left hand grip, as if to burrow into his skin.

A man's voice: "You saw nothing in Hiroshima. Nothing."

A woman's voice: "I saw everything."

Thus begins, in chorus real and surreal, a film about memory severe and sensual.

BLOW-UP (1966)

"A pop-culture icon that has become a cult classic. Antonioni's adaptation of Cortazar's short story is an engrossing study of imagery and one's perception of the image. In its time one of the most financially successful art films ever made."

— *movies.tvguide.com*

"It will be a crying shame if the audience that will undoubtedly be attracted to Michelangelo Antonioni's [film] because it has been denied a Production Code seal goes looking more for sensual titillation than for the good, solid substance it contains — and therefore will be distracted from recognizing the magnitude of its forest by paying attention to the comparatively few defoliated trees. This is a fascinating picture that has something real to say about the matter of personal involvement and emotional commitment in a jazzed-up, media-hooked-in world so cluttered with synthetic stimulations that natural feelings are overwhelmed."

— Bosley Crowther, *New York Times*, December 19, 1966

To read now Crowther's fascination with the film's statements about a "media-hooked world" and its "synthetic stimulations" is ironic indeed and illustrates that such concerns and warnings haven't issued a setback to the "clutter" after more than forty years. Sociologist Neil Postman, some fifteen years after this review, wrote *Amusing Ourselves to Death: Public Discourse in the Age of Entertainment*, and neither man, nor the Antonioni film, afforded so much as a crinkle to the rapid rush toward blissful seclusion. It is difficult to distinguish the hip fakery in gadget-attractive "mod" from developments of authentic value.

I ask Mr. Crowther's forgiveness for my selected moment. I was not looking for "sensual titillation" but for its allure in the reviewer's premise: I suspect it is Michelangelo Antonioni's as well.

Fashion photographer Thomas prepares his model and studio. Intimacy is suggested when his assistant Reg frees a window shade, and the ensuing darkness casts across the back of Verushka — a supermodel of the era — as she enters the medium gray no-seam stage of the studio. The model slips her shawl, and Thomas, with a handful of ostrich plumes, discards his boots.

A series of photographically implied jump cuts carry the beginnings of the session. Thomas drinks wine from a goblet as Reg reloads the camera. Eventually Thomas calls for a handheld SLR and moves around his model. "Give it to me now. Come on, that's good."

Thomas circles and nuzzles and commands as he snaps; and Verushka curls and swivels and self-handles her body and face, and leans into Thomas' lens.

THE *BLOW-UP* MOMENT: 0:09:01–0:09:57

In a straight-on master shot, Thomas calls for another camera and to his model gives an order: "On your back. On your back, go on."

Tangled moments of model and photographer propose oral and aggressive sex: "Stretch yourself, little lady. Great." "Keep it up." "Make it come. Great." "Head up. Head up." "Now for me, love, for me." "Now! Now! Yes! Yes! Yes!"

Thomas steps over his "little lady" and leaves her to the floor. Verushka, stretched out, is taking time to mend.

Following weeks of unremitting workday arguments over the movie's meaning(s), I walked along Greenwich Avenue on my way home from the Film Center Building when directly ahead, waiting to cross from the other side of the street, was Verushka. When the light set green, Verushka and I drew near. Eye contact was certain, and as we passed, we smiled to each other with a wee flirt. We never saw each other again.

2001: A SPACE ODYSSEY (1968)

"*2001* continues to annoy and delight audiences; for sheer spectacle, it may be unsurpassed. Its relatively low-tech special effects, masterfully engineered by Douglas Trumbull, remain more astonishing and persuasive than much of today's computer-generated gimmickry."
— *movies.tvguide.com*

"The movie opened yesterday at the Capitol.... It is so absorbed in its own problems, its use of color and space, its fanatical devotion to science-fiction detail, that it is somewhere between hypnotic and immensely boring. [Here is] a film in which infinite care, intelligence, patience, imagination and Cinerama have been devoted to what looks like the apotheosis of the fantasy of a precocious, early 1950's city boy. The whole sensibility is intellectual fifties child: chess games, body-building exercises, beds on the spacecraft that look like camp bunks. Richard Strauss music, Howard Johnson's birthday phone calls. In their space uniforms, the voyagers look like Jiminy Crickets."
— Renata Adler, *New York Times*, April 4, 1968

"Technically and imaginatively, it is staggering. It is also a poetic piece of sci-fi, made by a man who truly possesses the drives of both science and fiction. The grim joke is that life in 2001 is only faintly more gruesome in its details of sophisticated affluence than it is now. The citizens have forgotten how to joke and resist, just as they have forgotten how to chat, speculate, grow intimate, or interest one another. Separation from other people is total and unmentioned; [there are] no characters in the film who are sexually related. The film is hypnotically entertaining, but it is also rather harrowing."
— Penelope Gilliatt, *New Yorker*, April 13, 1968

This quintessential science fiction movie was found "boring" and "harrowing" by contemporaneous reviewers. Even the *TV Guide* database concedes an annoyance to moviegoers.

I've never been a sci-fi enthusiast. It has always seemed to me (since about age eleven) oxymoronic in characterization, more fittingly a genus of technological prophecy (tech-prof), a kind of wild guess-making (tech-guess) — in these respects, a futuristic fiction — fu-fi. In *2001*, I found myself far more gripped by the first sequence of prehistoric ape men, and while many moviegoers might agree that it is a "delight" in "sheer spectacle," for me Stanley Kubrick's brilliance is marked by the sensual.

In this prehistoric opening, a carnivorous aggressor dispatches an enemy and launches a skeletal club high to the sky. Without fastidiousness of aligned images, and with the spiraling bone beginning descent, a straightforward cut brings the future.

THE *2001: SPACE ODYSSEY* MOMENT: 00:19:49–00:21:18

The heaven and the earth and the sun; tubular craft and a spinning hub space station; a cosmos in peaceful benefit of a most delicately segued and set waltz by Johann Strauss. The manifestly male and female forms join in graceful connection: a sexual and sensual docking maneuver.

Stanley Kubrick preferred selections of existing music to original film scores, so it came as no surprise to hear familiar melodies. But I was gratifyingly comforted — and sensually stirred — that the introduction to outer space was not accompanied by dreadfully clichéd sounds of the Moog synthesizer.

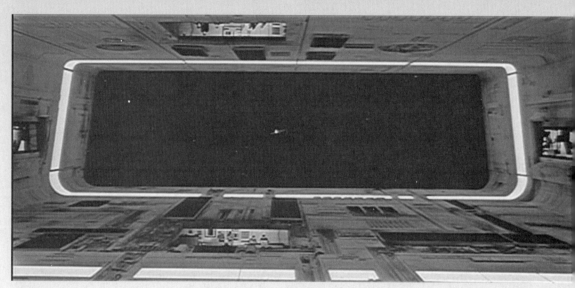

The attacks on the World Trade Center towers and the Pentagon on September 11, 2001, have forever altered visions of Kubrick's year.

ATLANTIC CITY (1980)

"Richly sad portraits of wasted American lives filtered through a European sensibility. Louis Malle, aided by a superb script from playwright John Guare, pulls off a minor coup here, celebrating his wounded characters even as he mercilessly reveals their dreams for the hopeless illusions they really are."

— *movies.tvguide.com*

"[The film] is a rich, gaudy cinema trip. Malle's fine new movie may be one of the most romantic and perverse ghost stories ever filmed, set not in a haunted castle but in a haunted city, the contemporary Atlantic City, a point of transit where the dead and living meet briefly."

— Vincent Canby, *New York Times*, April 3, 1981

"[The film] is a collaboration (between director, Louis Malle and playwright/screenwriter, John Guare) [wherein] Malle has entered into Guare's way of seeing — a mixture of observation, flights of invention, satire, perversity, anecdote, fable,... and depth of feeling. [Burt] Lancaster brings to the film the finest performance he has ever given."

— Pauline Kael, *New Yorker*, April 6, 1981

There is sensuality apparent in the reviews and database assessments. While the Louis Malle and John Guare collaboration respectfully "celebrates wounded characters" and in the end "reveals their dreams as illusions," its "romantic ghost story, set in a haunted city" also nudges notions of memories, assigned in the mind with such conviction — if not grandeur — that however "hopeless" a fairy tale, illusions sadly persist.

It is creatively concurrent that recollections of Malle and Guare initiated the story's characters, settings, and actions: from *Hints from Heloise* to exotic lemon washes; from a picture book showing an Atlantic City gangster convention in the 1920s to drug trafficking and age bracket prospects; from brainstorming at Resorts International's casino to beauty pageants.

THE *ATLANTIC CITY* MOMENT: 00:00:23–00:01:46

A small serrated knife slices through lemons that fill the screen. But for the quiet, concentrated cutting, and a few simple spurts of juice, the ambiance holds not a hush. A woman's hand — with a lemon held

in the palm — enters the frame and presses "play" on a radio-cassette machine bathed in a yellow light and held in the arm of a golden cupid that provides the fixture's base. The sweet tones of Maria Callas start from the miserly speakers.

Sally (Susan Sarandon) — in a medium close-up — begins, along the length of her right arm, to wash by readily squeezing fresh lemon juice from the sliced pieces. She wears a woven string-strap tank top and slips the right side off her shoulder so that she can cup that breast with the lemon-rich palm of her left hand. She repeats the cleansing with her other hand and arm. As she begins to lemon bathe her left breast, the camera slowly moves back, and we see with certainty that Sally is framed in a window.

She lemons her neck and upper chest, then again both breasts. Eventually the camera's zoom backs into another apartment, across the airshaft way, and we see Lou Pascal (Burt Lancaster) wearing a satin red bathrobe, watching Sally from his window. As Sally begins drying with a golden hand towel, Lou turns and lights a cigarette.

The explicit sensuality is less a feature of viewing Sally's breasts — they are obscured most of the time by objects on an inside window sill — than a voyeuristic secret we share with Lou; and, I expect, a reminder of special secrets we all keep unexposed.

Y TU MAMÁ TAMBIÉN (2001)

"A raunchy Mexican teen comedy with surprising depth and the nerve to confront subtexts that normally get short shrift in pictures aimed primarily at young men."
  —*movies.tvguide.com*

"The phrase translates as 'And your mama too.' The director, Alfonso Cuarón, works with a quicksilver fluidity, and the movie, which plays today and tomorrow at the New York Film Festival, is fast, funny, unafraid of sexuality and finally devastating. 'Mama' is finally a story of maturation [as two] hormonally consumed teenage boys who think of themselves as sophisticates [attend] to their appetites. Mr. Cuarón twists the narrative to peer at the latent homoeroticism that drives teenage sex-drive stories, something boys-to-men movies never deal with explicitly."
  — Elvis Mitchell, *New York Times*, October 6, 2002

The database's choice of "raunchy" as tonal characterization will likely attract "the young men" who will then find "subtexts" that they have little "nerve" to "confront." Positioning the genre as comedy might expose the reviewer's anxious encounters with content. The film *is* produced in Mexico.

The movie radiates with sexuality — neither vulgar nor crude or coarse — stimulated by postpubescent hormones and a glandular all-purpose experimental chemistry at the flanks of friends and relations:

Adolescents Tenoch and Julio voyage to Boca del Cielo (Heaven's
Mouth) — "a beach nobody knows about" — with Luisa, the (betrayed)
wife of Tenoch's older cousin, who the boys meet at a family wedding.

En route they rest over at a motel, with grounds hopelessly in need
of staff to tidy things up; an undersized pool is laden with dead leaves.

Luisa takes a room for herself, and Tenoch and Julio share another.
A close-up of a running shower head, then a pull back and tilt down
show Julio bathing. He calls to Tenoch: "Get me some shampoo."

THE *Y TU MAMÁ TAMBIÉN* MOMENT: 0:52:18–0:53:40

An above-angle medium shot is positioned behind Luisa: she sits on
the inside edge of a twin bed so that she faces the other bed and the
window beyond. She is whimpering into her hands, which cover her
face. The camera moves back to an off-screen call of a rooster.

The camera pans to the right to find Tenoch entering Luisa's room.
He is wrapped in a white towel. Tenoch apologizes, immediately deter-
mining that Luisa is distressed. But she welcomes him. "It's all right.
Come in."

Tenoch takes a few steps toward her. "Are you okay?"

The camera, lens wide, almost encompasses the entire motel room.
Tenoch has his back to the camera.

"Yes," comforts Luisa. "It must be the heat and the long drive."

"Could we borrow some shampoo?" Luisa touches her face, gliding her hair from it, but does not answer.

"You got some?" Tenoch tries again.

Although in long shot, we can tell that Luisa's gaze has shifted to Tenoch's middle, as she sweetly requests, "Take off the towel."

"What?"

"Take it off."

Tenoch nervously stalls. "The towel?"

"Yes, the towel."

Tenoch opens the towel and lets it drop; we can tell that he's covering his genitals with both hands, his buttocks exposed to the audience.

Luisa, who has been sitting on the first twin bed, her body turned leftward to see Tenoch, now moves to sit on the bed closest to the window, with a happier facing look at the boy. "Don't hide it."

Tenoch eases his hands to his side.

Luisa affectionately shakes her head in a giggle. "You get excited so fast."

"I guess," admits Tenoch.

Luisa instructs the boy to stroke himself, and then enticingly removes her blouse. "Do you want to see my tits?"

She calls Tenoch to her, her right arm extended to meet him. "Come over here. Closer."

The camera follows Tenoch. He stands before the seated Luisa. Her left hand caresses his behind; the fingers slide along the parting length of his cheeks. Tenoch's excitedly nervous breathing intensifies as Luisa tutors in oral pleasure.

The inexperienced male in the hands of an older, practiced, and enthusiastic female offers sensuality that is adorably charming in its innocence.

The camera continues its approach, moving past the sensual into explicit eventualities: Tenoch's gracelessly uncontrollable passions, while fastened crosswise on the slim twin bed, end with a speedy spurt —"Mamacita!"— and a feeble "I'm sorry."

TALK TO HER (2002)

"[Director] Pedro Almodóvar's transformation from rude boy into sophisticated interpreter of modern melodrama is remarkable, all the more so because he retained his gleeful willingness to affront conventional mores."

—*movies.tvguide.com*

"Like all great doomed affairs, the closing night presentation of the New York Film Festival is full of lovely sweet suffering. And when it's over, the realization of how much the movie means to you really sinks in; you can't get it out of your heart. It's the most mature work this director has ever brought to the screen.... [He has an] appreciation of flesh — no other director photographs skin so lovingly."

— Elvis Mitchell, *New York Times*, October 12, 2002

"Almodóvar's stories have always been improbable, even nutty, at the literal level but coherent and satisfying emotionally and poetically. A veteran of Madrid's gay cabaret scene and the city's funky comic-book culture, he relied on a fast pop tempo and abrupt transitions, and he was drawn to extravagance of every kind. Almodóvar was something new in movies — a soulful erotic entertainer of surpassing generosity. There's still a fabulist at large [in this film], but the attempt at psychological realism is new, and [the director] has brought an extraordinary calm to the surface of his work. The imagery is smooth and beautiful; the colors are soft-hued and blended. Past and present flow together; everything seems touched with a subdued and melancholy magic. A beautiful young ballet dancer who has been struck by a car has been in a coma for four years. Benigno [a male nurse] talks to her as he works."

— David Denby, *New Yorker*, November 25, 2002

While the *TV Guide* database tackles the director's creative epoch, Mitchell and Denby provide all necessary attributes that will ensure Pedro Almodóvar's prominent place in movie history.

By degree and ironies, the film is sensually affecting. The four central characters are at once romantic and platonic; distinctive sexual categories unfold amid idealization of desire and odd entanglements: Benigno, the caregiver to Alicia, the young comatose dancer; Marco, a freelance writer; and Lydia, a bullfighter, exotically androgynous and sexually irresistible.

A dance recital opens the movie — *Café Muller*, choreographed by
Pina Bausch — and its resonance divulges the story's many twists of fate.

Lydia's friends, family, associates, and lover, Marco, gather prior
to her next fight. An abrasive discussion about a newspaper account
of nuns raped by missionaries in Africa adjoins a curious close-up that
initiates the scene: a woman brings together candles, Christ picture
cards, an image of the virgin, and rosary beads to create an altar atop a
narrow side table — a safeguard for Lydia in the arena.

"If you can't trust a missionary, what's to become of us?"

Marco, in matter-of-fact intonations, furnishes a historical perspective, "They used to rape the local women. Because of AIDS, they
started raping the nuns." "I'm sure not all of them are rapists," someone cautions. "No," Marco updates, "some of them are pedophiles."

Lydia enters from a bathroom. It is reported to her that the bulls
look big, "over 1,000 pounds." She wears a blue bathrobe of orange
and white polka and oblong dots. She disrobes, presenting a trim body
in black brassiere and white ribbed body tights.

THE *TALK TO HER* MOMENT: 0:22:22–0:23:31

An extreme close-up of brightly colored fabrics and textures sets in
motion exuberant costuming: a close-up of an athletically charged leg
extends across the width of center frame. An assistant's hand relaxes
below Lydia's heel as pink long-stockings unfurl over white tights,
ending just above the knee. The assistant's hands slide a pale gray garter
up the calf, and Lydia clasps it while the assistant's hands concentrate
on softening wrinkles in the pink stocking. A graceful flower, also in
pink, decorates the outside of the leg at the lower calf. A bold cut
brings a close-up of elegantly embroidered pants — heavy gold threads
weave a vine and petals along a cocoa brown fabric, gem spotted with
red floral eyes — and the assistant's hands leisurely guide Lydia's pink-
clad feet from the design-elaborate ankle openings. The camera pans
right and tilts slightly as Lydia stands. The assistant passes between
her and the camera, clearing a view of Lydia's white-tighted middle; a
strong seam runs vertically from her navel to vagina, the upper edge
of the pants held at her thighs. The assistant circles behind Lydia, and
together their four hands slither the pant legs upward. A wide padded

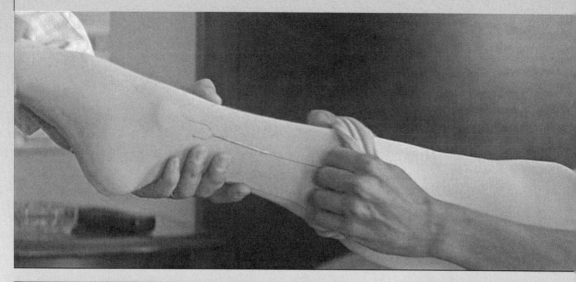

waistband wraps Lydia's abdomen, as the assistant elevates the pants, boosting Lydia off her feet.

An extreme close-up displays new details of the superbly crafted pants as fingers with a buttonhook clasp them at Lydia's ankles.

Then a master shot: Lydia stands full body in center frame. Chinese red drapes allow narrow columns of light into the room. Her assistant carefully lifts the matching outer jacket from a simple wooden chair: actions indicate in manner a delicate jacket, substantially shaped in weight. Standing behind Lydia, the jacket steered outward and aligned with her arms, the assistant wishes, "Good luck," tugging the collar and her hair tailpiece in place. Her furry matador hat rests on the chair.

In a final medium shot, the assistant yanks the jacket forward. Lydia's hair is tense to her head, her face solemn. The textural elegance of her costume; her agile and edgy manner; and the pleasured promise in the dresser's touch convey sensuality in a coaxing to covert sex.

Be regular and orderly in your life so that you may be violent and original in your work.

— *Gustave Flaubert*

PROVOCATIVE

Provocative is a somewhere between Sensual and Disturbing: It is the controversial ignited by sex, violence, and language.

Father Adelfio — the village priest in *Cinema Paradiso* — highlights a moment of hilarious censorship: The priest holds a private screening of the latest movie to arrive in the village. Alfredo operates the projector. The light is illuminated out the open mouth of a carved lion high above the auditorium. The priest is equipped with a small-handled bell at the ready. Both romantically gentle lip taps and lustful mouth clinches get a ring; and Alfredo slips small pieces of white paper onto the take-up spooling reel as indicator of a moment that must not be viewed. Young Totò secretly attends the priest's viewings and can barely "abstain" from laughter. The missing moments are eventually and joyfully joined in plot line to Alfredo and Totò's friendship.

At the Paradiso one night, a discouraged grown-up shouts, "Twenty years I've gone to movies and never saw a kiss!"

Social satirist Lenny Bruce wondered aloud why the electrifyingly pleasurable connection that makes possible our arrival into this world is far more shocking to the public's well-being than is the viciousness that imperils our stay.

I AM CURIOUS — YELLOW (1967)

"[It was] seized by U.S. Customs, guaranteeing not only a trial (could a film widely admired in Europe bring about moral collapse in the United States?), but also zealous highbrow support and palpitating pietistic outrage. Norman Mailer proclaimed *Yellow* 'one of the most important pictures I have ever seen in my life,' while Rex Reed called it 'vile and disgusting.' Perhaps no other film in cinema history sparked so much critical and popular mayhem as Vilgot Sjöman's *I Am Curious — Yellow*, only to be consigned to nearly instantaneous oblivion."

— Gary Giddins, "Still Curious," Criterion Collection, March 10, 2003, *www.criterion.com*

The film remains controversial (enough) so that it was nearly impossible — apart from Internet sites — to locate accounts in conventional periodicals, let alone in the *VideoHound's Independent Film Guide* (revised and expanded) or the *2005 Film and Video Companion*, which describes more than 3,500 movies beginning in 1930.

Curiously, the film's "neglect for more than three decades," as Giddins describes in his review, may have less to do with the (comparatively few) scenes of full nudity or sexual contact — a "promise" of pubic hair, a follow-on of critic Rex Reed's ridicule of director Vilgot Sjöman, did lure movie-goers — than with its sweeping defiance of political, social, religious, and economic establishments. It arrived at the height of the protest era.

In keeping with the on-hand film crew documenting Lena's ventures and intimacies and Sweden's visitors — such as Dr. Martin Luther King Jr. and Soviet poet Yevgeny Yevtushenko — the director and the entire production team escort Lena, on retreat to the country, rapt in Eastern renunciation and meditation, so that, attended by twanging Western jazz and Eastern strings, they all practice yoga poses even while the camera crew "fusses" with the equipment.

Lena, wrapped in flowered fabric with breasts bared, becomes frustrated while struggling to fold and overlie her legs: "No. I can't do it!" The director rests his shoulders in the grass and, lifting his legs straight up in the air, instructs, "Have a look. Look, then."

Lena's bourgeois (and deceiving) lover Börje speedily appears in his MG convertible.

Lena is still practicing yoga, this time tilted back on her shoulders, her ass aimed upward, with legs together, extended over her head, her large breasts gravity-directed onto her face. What might this yoga position be called?

As the MG noisily brakes, Lena scuttles through a side window and retrieves a shotgun, which had rested across a farmer-style table-bench shrine with a photograph of Dr. King, labeled "Nonviolence: Martin Luther King and Lena": *I Am Curious — Yellow* was made prior to Dr. King's assassination.

Börje, wearing large shades, enters the house to find her. "Lena.... Lena?"

THE *I AM CURIOUS — YELLOW* MOMENT: 1:18:05–1:20:10

Lena returns outside and loads the gun, then runs — armed and jiggling — back into the house, sneaking up on Börje and poking the barrel to his back. His body lifts, startled, and he surrenders both hands into the air; but suddenly he makes a run for it! The score plunks a jokey rendition of an Appalachian banjo melody.

Lena ineptly fires off one shot; it misses, but Börje stops and slowly turns to face her. His chest is exposed as his fleeing dash had thrust his shirt inelegantly across a shoulder. The music quick-shifts into satirical sci-fi or horror tones.

Lena approaches Börje with shotgun ready, and as they begin circling, the tunes mingle. At a turn of 180 degrees, Lena jerks her head in anger, "Get lost!"

Börje slowly walks to Lena. He removes his sunglasses, and his eyes add to a little smirk on his lips. He grabs hold of the barrel, tossing the gun away, and presses Lena to the ground. The camera tilts downward with them; Lena's nipples hold the lower edge of the frame. Börje flips each end of her flowered wrap upward and pursues Lena's middle with his face.

A dissolve brings a master shot (ever so slightly looking down) of conflict relief and love-making respite. Lena and Börje are nude, pressed to each other in leafy sun and shadow. Börje's head is at screen right.

One hand moves to Lena's thigh; the other, with arm under Lena's legs, clasps her lower calf. Lena's head, to screen left, naps at Börje's soft member, the fingers of her left hand gently gathered in his pubic hair.

A close-up of Börje. "You were hard to find."

A close-up of Lena. "Have you been searching a lot?"

Then, a most sweetly mischievous movie moment: Curiously, the iconic image of *Yellow*. Lena gingerly kisses Börje's penis, her eyes closed, an exhale in a delicate sigh.

The adjective "flaccid" is customary when describing Börje's kissed penis. I myself wouldn't think to add a qualifier other than "erect" — if it were accurate. To fuss over this one penis is twice as silly: The eye makes no contact with the camera.

It is of value to take note that the film's director, Vilgot Sjöman, was a protégé of Ingmar Bergman, that none of his other films were ever distributed in the United States, and that the filmmaker died on April 9, 2006.

MIDNIGHT COWBOY (1969)

"[This movie] was the only 'X'-rated picture ever to win an Oscar for Best Picture. The rating was later changed to an 'R' and, by today's standards, might almost be considered a 'PG-13.' The film presents New York at its seamiest, and though it includes one very funny parody of a Bohemian party, it's mostly pretty downbeat stuff."
— *movies.tvguide.com*

"[The film] often seems to be exploiting its material for sensational or comic effect, but it is ultimately a moving experience that captures the quality of a time and a place. It's not a movie for the ages, but having seen it you won't ever again feel detached as you walk down West 42d Street, avoiding the eyes of the drifters, stepping around the little islands of hustlers, and closing your nostrils to the smell of rancid griddles."
— Vincent Canby, *New York Times*, May 26, 1969

"Director John Schlesinger relies a lot on close-ups, perhaps to signify the intense, vivid impressions of the naïve nineteen- or twenty-year-old, under the influence of movies and television, and, also, to suggest the dimensions of the boy's fantasy, which has to do with cashing in on his Southwestern virility as the savior of New York's sex-starved women."
— Susan Lardner, *New Yorker*, May 31, 1969

The movie effortlessly fits this section if only for the historic sway of a Best Picture achievement adjoining an "X" rank — and that provokes a place in this book. Protagonist Joe Buck emigrates via long-distance bus, bringing potent plans to use his "Southwestern virility" in the Big Apple: "The men [in New York] are mostly tutti-fruttis."

In thinking back on my first viewing, I did recollect that premise and have long considered memorable the discordant alliance of Joe and Enrico "Ratso" Rizzo, a pickpocket, street thief, and hustler in the last pangs of tuberculosis. My summer 2009 viewing, forty years after seeing the original release, accessed unexpected ingredients: The film's atmosphere outdoes "New York at its seamiest" — likely outdoing the despair of Dickens' London. The "very funny parody of a Bohemian party" manages to be neither funny nor parodic.

Canby's proposition that "you won't ever again feel detached as you walk down West 42d Street, avoiding the eyes of the drifters, stepping around the little islands of hustlers" might be true, but the bleakness of the movie does not allow the lack of detachment to lead to empathy or compassion. The story is so uninviting as to be understated by the phrase "pretty downbeat stuff."

I did not recall the extensive backstory of Joe Buck's life or the intricate cross-cutting along with flash-forward structures.

Townsend P. Locke (from Chicago and thirty years Joe's senior) introduces himself in a Times Square arcade. "I'm here on a paper manufacturer's convention and frankly... to have a little fun, damn it." "Towny" — as he asks to be called — is suitably dressed for a midwestern salesman: gray suit; white shirt; a burnished lizard-green tie that matches his green wool scarf; and a gray fedora.

A cut brings Joe and Towny in a brisk walk along an after-dark midtown street. Towny talks to the tempo in their stride and sales pitch. "This is my first night here, and I'd feel privileged if you'd have dinner with me. There's a little French restaurant not too far from here. Italian restaurant? Does that appeal to you? Don't worry about how you're dressed. They know me. Besides I'll tell them you're here with the rodeo. There's always a rodeo in town, damn it." Towny hastens the pickup: "Damn it all, we can't do that. I'm expecting a phone call at the hotel."

A cut takes us to a medium shot of Towny: He is on the telephone, seated alongside a lamp, just in front of a photo of a well winter-dressed woman. We can guess the portrait's identity at once; Towny with salesman enthusiasm speaks up, "Mama?"

Joe Buck is in the bathroom. His suede tasseled jacket is off; he wears a deep blue-magenta cowboy shirt, embroidered with white and yellow threads, a black bandanna neatly tied mid-neck. Joe confers with himself in the medicine chest mirror, preparing a money-making approach to the salesman: "Listen, Towny, did I tell you I got this sick kid on my hands?" Towny is in the mirror as well, his reflection blurred but certain: He is behind Joe in conversation with his mama, sitting on the hotel bed. As Joe works up his wiles, cross-cutting moves the story forward: Joe struggling to get the desperately ill Rizzo downstairs and out the building, into a taxi to the Port Authority Terminal, and onboard a Florida-bound bus.

A close-up of poor Rizzo's dragging shoes conveys Joe's direct words to Towny: "What you want?"

THE *MIDNIGHT COWBOY* MOMENT: 1:39:40–1:42:15

A cut brings us a camera move left, past Joe's tight-assed pants. The camera rests as the composition reveals Towny sitting exactly in line with Joe's crotch as Joe asks, "What you got me up here for?"

Towny is pained by ambivalence. "Oh Joe, it's difficult. You're a nice person. I should never have asked you up here. You're a lovely person, really."

Towny's fingers are clasped, very much in prayer; he "confesses": "Oh God, I loathe life. I loathe it." He asks Joe to leave but to promise a return tomorrow. "I'm goin' to Florida tomorrow." Towny takes a chain and medallion from around his neck and hands it to Joe. "I want to give you a present for your trip. I want you to have it. You don't have to be a Catholic. Saint Christopher is the patron saint of all travelers. I want you to have it for helping me be good."

There is no "thank you" from Joe, only a fast "I gotta have money."

"Yes, of course. Wait here." Towny walks to the night table and gets his wallet from the narrow drawer, lifting a single ten dollar bill. Joe is

directly on him. "I gotta have more than ten. I gotta have fifty-seven dollars."

Joe wants the wallet, "Get out of my way," and gut punches Towny, who falls yet clings to the drawer and his wallet. Joe is adamant but polite. "Let go of that table, please, sir." Towny fights him, begging, "Please. No, please." Joe smacks him in the face. "I deserved that. I brought this on myself, I know I did. My nose is bleeding, isn't it?"

Then cross-cuts of the sickly Rizzo and the nose-bleeding Towny merge, and Joe wallops the old salesman. Towny's dentures fall from his mouth. "Oh Joe, thank you." With all the cash, Joe speeds for the door. The room telephone has come uncradled, and a voice from the hotel switchboard can be heard at a cross-cut to Joe and Rizzo making their way down the aisle of a bus. "Operator. Number please."

An extreme close-up of the prone bald head of Towny as the operator's inquiry continues, "Number please," while a pan to the right rack-focuses on Joe as he puts on his buckskin jacket and black cowboy hat. In a slight whisper, Towny explains, "No, I wasn't calling anyone," but Joe hurries to grab the phone and jerks the cord from the wall. Joe stands over Towny, who continues in a whisper, "I wasn't calling anyone. I wasn't calling anyone. Oh Joe. Joe. Joe."

Joe Buck jams the telephone into Towny's mouth.

The pitiable Mr. Townsend and the frantic Joe, "a nice person... a lovely person, really," assemble a moment so reckless — so pathetic and so ghastly — that its memory provokes unshakable horror.

JU DOU (1990)

"[Here, in his second feature, Director] Zhang Yimou... delves once more into the past for... a haunting story of illicit love set in 1920s China. [Yimou and other] 'Fifth Generation' filmmakers began a new wave in Chinese cinema by emphasizing the visual and aural qualities of film rather than traditional dramatic and literary elements. *Ju Dou* is no exception to this trend."

— *movies.tvguide.com*

"Mr. Zhang is a social critic who choreographs actions and images at the expense of emotions. Individual scenes jump out in brilliantly conceived moments. Beaten by her impotent husband because she has not borne a son, Ju Dou appeals to the lonely Tian Qing. When she discovers a peephole through which he watches her bathe, she is at first appalled. Later, she uses his voyeurism as a way to display the bruises that cover her body. By Western standards, it is a scene of extraordinary discretion and a mere shade of titillation. But by Chinese standards both the character and the film are startlingly bold.... 'Ju Dou' is an intellectually and artistically brave film."

— Caryn James, *New York Times*, September 22, 1990

"Ju Dou was the first Chinese film to be nominated for an Academy Award. The Chinese government fought the nomination for the film,

> which had effectively been banned in its own country.... [The] director's interpretation of Liu Heng's novel-based screenplay is masterful; it was his wonderfully cinematic decision to transplant the story into a dye factory. [The film] lingers in the mind, both for its compelling narrative and its deeply disturbing emotional landscape."
> — Monica Sullivan, *Independent Film Guide*, 2nd Edition

The director's background includes an experience in a textile factory and likely endorses the critical selection of "place" fully integrated with the characters and the story. It is one of Zhang's ongoing accomplishments. His first feature, *Red Sorghum*, which closed the 1988 New York Film Festival, was located in a wine factory.

Though accounts in outlines vary in designating the relationship between Tian Qing and Ju Dou's husband — they are close relatives, or an adoptive parent and son, or an uncle and nephew — Tian Qing refers to Yang Jin-shan as "Uncle" and Ju Dou as "Auntie." When the factory's pack animal takes ill, Jin-shan accompanies it to a veterinarian in another village. Ju Dou presses Tian Qing to take her.

The nephew avoids eye contact as Ju Dou removes a banana from his mouth and embraces his bare chest. Their hands are entangled and blue stained from their work. Ju Dou announces, "It is virgin and for you."

THE *JU DOU* MOMENT: 0:28:35–0:29:15

Primitive wind instruments initiate a provocative aural sensuality, replicating a harrowing choral ritual, simultaneous to a mounting "throbbing" of the factory's beam works. Tian Qing unlocks Ju Dou's hands from his chest and turns, pushing her backward and down. Red cloth drapes her face.

No matter Western standards of discretion (or titillation), nor the provocation stimulated in Chinese sensibilities, the object representations in liquid, texture, and color display a female arousal that outstrips the modesty of eroticism in its forceful pleasure. Ju Dou tumbles back; her lips part in an open smile, letting in a cascade of invigorating spray. Tian Qing is purged at the moment of penetration: the strokes of Ju Dou's partner are served by a kicked-free flywheel and pounding timbers, as blood-red cloth spins upward from a woven vessel, vigorously

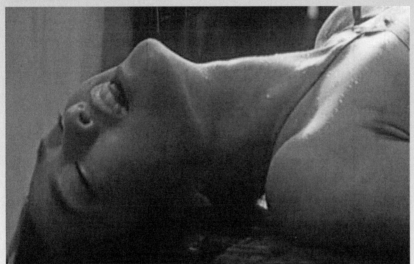

discharging back into a vat of dye — all in a series of smartly juxta-posed images and sounds rhythmically swathed to "linger in the mind."

I am unsure of Caryn James' point concerning the director's choreo-graphing "actions and images at the expense of emotions." I don't know that the actions and images can expend emotions. The notion is a cinematic contradiction.

Zhang Yimou has completed several highly commercial movies, and the Chinese government "promoted" him creative director of the Beijing Olympics. I trust the world has not lost a brave artist-provocateur.

UNDER THE SAND (2000)

"A haunting tale of obsession and loss. Professor Marie Drillon and her husband (Jean) of 25 years are spending the summer at their cottage near the beach. [Her] husband announces he's going in for a swim. He never returns. [The director] tend[s] to press a point long after it's been made, but this exploration of devastating loss and our imperfect mechanisms for dealing with it resonates with a pathos that moves well beyond sadness."
— *movies.tvguide.com*

"At one point the ghost of her husband, a hulking cuckold from beyond the grave, watches over her [while she is in bed with an architect friend]; she smiles at Jean as she comes. This is more tender than creepy, and, for all the formality of [Director François] Ozon's approach, [*Under the Sand*] is wonderfully liquid. In the final shot Marie runs hopefully toward a distant man on a beach. Ozon, ruthless to the last, waits till she is almost there, then cuts her off."
— Anthony Lane, *New Yorker*, May 21, 2001

The database envelops a quick synopsis. The movie holds a "haunting" atmosphere and has been represented as "a dream-like erotic mystery." It is, as well, a film likely inaccessible to those under forty years of age: cyclic experiences that, over decades, imprint repetitively precise memo-ries, reinforcing outlooks and prospects, can, when life's unforeseen appears, pervert expectations (and assumptions) into a kind of emotional bafflement. Empathy for such consequences seldom exists in the young.

During this writing, my wife and I were making preparations for our visit to her family home in Vermont, shut to the severe winter months and opened when we can stay for at least a week's time to get things up, running, and, if need be, repaired. Though the Drillons' home does not compel the shutting requirements of a Vermont house — winters "near Lit et Mix" can't compare to Mount Holly's and the necessary plumbing precautions of double-digit below-zero temperatures — the movie's opening sequence is comparably connected: a long drive; highway rest stop; getting there; unbolting a door; opening shuttered windows to new air; stripping off protective sheets from the couch; and gathering wood for a fire, offering warmth and an end to seasonal dampness.

Marie Drillon, severely sad and unable to be free of recurring denials that husband, Jean, is gone, nevertheless invites architect friend — and captivated suitor — Vincent for dinner. Earlier Marie and Vincent had made love at his place, initially interrupted by Marie's uncontrollable giggles. "I'm sorry. It's just... you're so light. It's not a bad thing. I'm just not used to it" — the allusion, of course, to hefty Jean.

At her place, she readies a pasta dinner. The two share wine and the romantic warmth of a fireplace. The proceedings and easy menu also render memories of the movie's opening sequence.

THE *UNDER THE SAND* MOMENT: 01:06:48–01:08:52

Marie, in two close-ups (the second tighter), cleanses her face with a soft astringent cloth. There is self-investigation in her eyes. A cut to a master shot instantly reveals Vincent in bed with a book — another reminder of Jean — and Marie approaching in screen right. She climbs into bed. Vincent smiles, mentioning that the book was "found by the bed." Marie, with a thin kiss, says, "Good night," and turns, facing her side of the bed. Vincent shuts off a small lamp and, turning to Marie, he kisses her shoulder and cuddles alongside.

"Did you set the alarm?" she asks. Vincent slowly lifts his head, "What alarm?"

A cut brings a divided frame: half black on screen left; the right is constructed with a wide white molding centered and vertical, and to its side, the clam-patterned fabric wallpaper of Marie's bedroom.

Jean leans in from "behind" the black of the left frame into the right half. There is a pleasantness expressed in his eyes and mouth. We can hear subdued breathing. A cut brings an above-angle close-up of Marie and Vincent. Her eyes are closed, and his face is secured to

her neck. Vincent begins to thrust up and down, his breathing now obvious. Marie opens her eyes and focuses to screen right. She grants intermittent smiles and a few sighs. The scene cuts back to Jean, now thoroughly taking pleasure in the moment. Gasps begin coming more rapidly and forcefully. Marie shuts her eyes, her head tilting upward into the pillow; when they open, Jean is vanished. Marie's eyes close again, and she and Vincent gently kiss.

Jean's voyeuristic pleasure is that of a ghost, yet nonetheless (in the light of movie magic) it rouses feelings about eternal fidelity, obligations to intimate commitment, and a perpetual self-doubting in worlds both physical and spiritual.

Laughter is wine for the soul — laugh soft, or loud and deep, tinged through with seriousness. Comedy and tragedy step through life together, arm in arm.... Once we can laugh, we can live.

— Sean O'Casey

UPROARIOUS

My mother instituted a street-crossing prohibition that was effective till age nine. It exacted small inconvenience, what with pedestrians aplenty all positively cheery when I'd ask, "Mister, will you take me across the street?" The regulation abridged some self-confidence when many friends were, by age seven or eight, granted full access throughout the neighborhood and my mother said "No" to newly "licensed" playmates guiding me from street to street. At times friends would wait with me at a corner for an attending adult to take my hand so that all the gang could cross together; on other occasions they would cross and wait at the next corner. And so my mother regularly posted herself outside Public School 147 at Gouverneur and Henry Street to get me home safely when school let out.

Another, and allied, concern of my mother's was that I was so perilously slight — nearly invisible to truck traffic — so that on each and every morning, she would prepare a breakfast drink of raw eggs, heavy cream, and granulated sugar whisked frothy. When the breakfast-bulky recipe proved ineffective, my mother supplemented her menu: She began meeting me at 3:00 p.m. at the Gouverneur Street and East Broadway side of P.S. 147 and, instead of heading home, we'd detour so that she could order up a bite for me at Dave's Luncheonette.

Daily, for many months, a scrambled egg on a buttered roll and calorie-crammed coffee — the cup heavily creamed and considerately sugared — was served to me by Dave himself. Dave and Francis Lazar's eating place swarmed streetside on weekends and was, even during the work week, an animated neighborhood hangout, sitting at the corner of East Broadway and Montgomery Street, making it on-foot accessible to four pairs of aunts and uncles and nine first cousins. You might say that Dave's Luncheonette catered to pedestrian tastes — but don't.

My aunt Ida — twin sister to my father — married Ben Chasen, adding an Uncle Benny who, with my aunt and their daughters,

Roseann and Helene, lived on Henry Street, only steps from Dave's. Uncle Benny was a showman-clown at the end of the burlesque and vaudeville era and seldom held a 9 to 5 job. His height, quite minor, was nearly matched by his width, and upon his chunky shoulders sat an effortlessly funny, (very) large face. In 1948 he appeared (portraying a gangster named Ben) in a Howard Hawks movie, *A Song Is Born*, from a story by Billy Wilder and featuring Danny Kaye, Virginia Mayo, Louis Armstrong, Lionel Hampton, Benny Goodman, and Tommy Dorsey.

Uncle Benny would spot himself on the corner of Dave's Luncheonette and gather every child at hand to "Go for a ride on a choo-choo-train." With the splendor of a three-ring tumbler, Benny would place three cigarettes — one at a breathtaking time — across his bottom lip and, with equivalent finesse, light them with separate and slowly struck matches, extinguished with magical flair. He'd then lift all three cigarettes with a jut of his lip, flipping them, still lit, into his mouth, and after several large chews, he'd announce, "The choo-choo train is ready." A line of children would form and follow him along the sidewalk, as Uncle Benny mimicked a train whistle, chugged his arms forward and back, and puffed white smoke through his puckered mouth.

One afternoon, before I could finish my egg sandwich, customers unexpectedly dashed to Dave's East Broadway window. My mother and I joined in. Uncle Benny had thrown himself to the pavement in front of two men crossing Montgomery Street and started bubbling at the mouth. The men hurried to his side. One cradled Benny's big head; the other sought assurance, "Sir, are you all right?" Inside, Dave's patrons pressed close to the glass — a memory revisited after more than sixty years, envisioned as if watching a scene on an advanced model Hi-Def flat-screen TV, or maybe on a smallish art house movie screen, also well ahead of its time. Uncle Benny urgently pointed to the luncheon-ette and beseeched, "Quick, get me a malted!"

Everyone, including the two "Samaritans," enjoyed the tumult, especially when Dave made Benny a malted on the house. I hold fond admiration still for Chaplin, Keaton, and Hardy and Laurel — enrich-ing childhood clowns — yet, all the same, I quickly picture my Uncle Benny, an uproarious street performer.

By the early 1950s Ben Chasen was a featured funny man on Saturday night television, and over the next decade, he appeared on several daytime children's shows, bringing good laughs to viewers at home and bigheartedly sharing his happy success with family and friends.

One weekend evening, Uncle Benny treated a large gathering to the upscale — and well uptown of the Pageant — Chinese restaurant the House of Chan. I was holding my mother's hand at the neon illuminated entranceway, taking in the C-H-A-N, when I thought instantly that my Aunt Ida and Uncle Benny (CHAseN) were now proprietors of a very fine Chinese establishment.

BUTCH CASSIDY AND THE SUNDANCE KID (1969)

"Although much of its freshness has faded, this still amusing film reinvented the Western for a new generation."
— *movies.tvguide.com*

"[The two] were real-life, turn-of-the-century outlaws who, in 1905, packed up their saddlebags, along with Sundance's mistress (a schoolteacher named Etta Place) and left the shrinking American West to start a new life, robbing banks in Bolivia. According to the movie which opened yesterday at the Penthouse and Sutton Theatres, their decline and fall was the sort of alternately absurd and dreamy saga that might have been fantasized by Truffaut's Jules and Jim and Catherine — before they grew up.... Butch and Sundance have the physical graces of classic Western heroes, but all four feet are made of silly putty. When they try to rob a train and blow open its safe, the dynamic charge destroys not only the safe but also the entire baggage car. When they can escape from a posse only by jumping from a high cliff into a raging rapids below, Sundance must admit ruefully that he doesn't know how to swim."
— Vincent Canby, *New York Times*, September 25, 1969

"It is a facetious Western,... a spin-off from *Bonnie and Clyde*, and everybody in it talks comical. Maybe were supposed to be charmed when this affable, loquacious outlaw Butch and his silent 'dangerous' buddy Sundance blow up trains, but how are we supposed to feel when they go off to Bolivia, sneer at the country, and start shooting up poor Bolivians?"
— Pauline Kael, *New Yorker*, September 27, 1969

"Where are the romantic idols who made their reputations on their appeal to women, the John Barrymores and Leslie Howards to whom women offered themselves in marriage? To Robert Redford and Paul Newman, who might conceivably be thought of as their successors, women, when they bother, send only billet-doux…. Instead of playing opposite beautiful women in love stories of civilized narratives, they play opposite each other in *Butch Cassidy and the Sundance Kid*, and romance takes on a whole new twist. They are on their way to becoming the Myrna Loy-William Powell of the seventies."

— Molly Haskell, "The Woman's Film," *Reverence to Rape*, 1974

The Western as genre is likely the most timid in category, clinched only (it appears) by regional hats and horses. The reviewer comments convey a neglect of tonal atmosphere and relevant genus. For the most part, this movie stirs together the all-purpose appeal of a live-action adventure with a charm scarcely achievable in the perils of Looney Tunes animation. All in all, Molly Haskell's misgivings sound a pop-cultured disappointment that the organs of leading men might be lost to female openings forever: the handsome Hollywood star mislaid.

Butch (Paul Newman) and Sundance (Robert Redford) are chased, trailed, and tracked by the Pinkerton posse, led by Joe LeFors, "the toughest lawman." No matter the outlaws' brainy ruses, the man in the white skimmer (straw hat) is always on course; and in due course, he has them trapped on a cliff shelf high above a rapid river.

THE *BUTCH CASSIDY AND THE SUNDANCE KID* MOMENT: 0:58:49–1:00:16

Cassidy burdens Sundance with their tight spot: "Kid, the next time I say let's go someplace like Bolivia, let's go someplace like Bolivia" (I might have said, "with their pickle," but that would even more stalwartly confirm Haskell's regrets.)

Sundance loads his revolver to fight it out. "Ready?"

Butch gazes into space beyond the cliff. "No. We'll jump."

Sundance adds his gaze, and a POV looks down from way up high, presenting boulders both jagged and huge, and yes, the running river too.

As if by inveterate request, the outlaws convert to the comedic banter of vaudeville:

"Like hell we will."

"No, it'll be okay," pledges Cassidy as he removes his jacket. "If the water's deep enough, and we don't get squished to death. They'll never follow us."

"How do you know?" doubts Sundance.

Cassidy is nimble with logic, "Would you make a jump like that you didn't have to?"

Sundance plugs the discussion. "I have to, and I'm not gonna."

Cassidy won't take "No" for an answer. "Well, we got to, otherwise we're dead. They're gonna have to go back down the same way they come. Come on!"

The Kid would rather do battle. "Just one clear shot, that's all I want."

Cassidy hugs the Kid's elbow with assurance. "Come on.... We got to."

The Kid pulls free. "Get away from me. I want to fight them."

Butch reckons, "They'll kill us."

The Kid's not convinced. "Maybe."

Butch is. "You want to die?"

Sundance shrugs the barrel of his revolver toward the cliff edge. "Do you?"

Butch unfastens his gun belt. "All right. I'll jump first."

The Kid is definite. "No."

Cassidy reasons, "Then you jump first."

The unambiguous Kid. "No, I said."

Butch is very nearly stumped. "What's the matter with you?"

The Kid shouts his confession, "I can't swim!" then confirms the fact with a rueful nod.

Cassidy can't restrain himself — he busts out laughing uproariously. "Why, you crazy? The fall will probably kill you!"

For ten seconds the two outlaws urge their nerve. The "shushing-whoosh" of the rapids' ambiance swells in evidence.

Sundance tersely braces. "Oh-oh ... oh-oh-oh-oh." Then Cassidy and Kid grip each end of a gun belt and they soar: "Oh-oh-oh. Shhhiiiiiiit!"

WHERE'S POPPA? (1970)

"The ultimate black comedy about difficult Jewish mothers, *Where's Poppa?* can be very funny, but suffers from the non-stop barrage of jokes."
— *movies.tvguide.com*

"If [this movie], which opened yesterday at the Coronet Theater, doesn't succeed all the time, or even most of the time, it succeeds often enough, if only by energy and will, to satisfy a taste for comedy that has not had much nourishment this season. And occasionally, when invention, which is in long supply, and execution, which isn't always, get properly together, [we have here] a desperately funny film."
— Roger Greenspun, *New York Times*, November 11, 1970

Roger Greenspun does contribute a synopsis following his opening comments on comedy. The straightforward premise is easy: New
York attorney Gordon Hocheiser (George Segal) lives with his mother
(Ruth Gordon), who is senile and yet mischievously scheming to ruin
her son's romantic relationships.

Greenspun goes on to describe the "energy and will" of director
Carl Reiner's work: "The situation will seem familiar enough to post-
Oedipal America." The simplicity of the premise ought to have been
permitted, but the script is abundant with subplots that, with a "barrage
of jokes," offer up dozens of gags far afield of silly and often inter-
rupt the unfussy (yet messy) tale of a Jewish boy fixed to his mother:
a promise to his late father, and dread of mortal guilt, keep Gordon
from delivering Mrs. Hocheiser to a nursing home.

Beyond a feel for the Oedipal attributes, an audience would do well
to have been under psychoanalytic supervision or in analysis for a few
decades, or at least to possess an urban mindset or the acquaintances
of a few Jews. Here is comedy that so briskly cultivates the contentious
that its provocations befit the uproarious.

Gordon meets, hires, and falls for a lovely nurse. Before nurse
(Louise) Callan (Trish Van Devere) meets Mrs. Hocheiser, Gordon
prepares his very tiny, age-demented mom, who's been trying to watch
a prize fight on her television set in her nailed-shut bedroom. "Mom,
there's somebody I want you to meet.... Ma, there's a girl here that I
want you to meet. She's very nice. I like her very much. She's going to
help me take care of you. She's not just another nurse, Mom. It means
a lot to me, Ma. And I want you to know that if you mess this one up
for me, I'm going to punch your fucking heart out!"

Gordon confirms that his mother understands, "Got it?" and kisses
her sweetly on the forehead.

No! That was not the moment.

THE *WHERE'S POPPA?* MOMENT: 0:55:34–0:56:16

Nurse Callan arrives with Chinese take-out, a cuisine common to
Jewish get-togethers and a "cooked-up" twofold joke seeing as Callan
is gentile, or in Yiddish, *shiksa*: an ill-mannered reference to a non-Jew-
ish woman. While Gordon makes serving preparations in the kitchen,

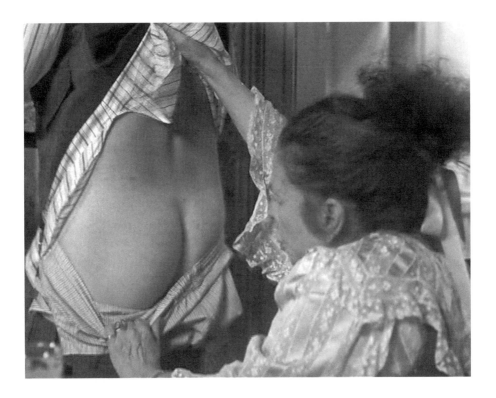

the nurse joins Mrs. Hocheiser at the modest dining table. Mother (confused?) identifies the nurse as Gordon and asks that "he" not sit in Poppa's chair. Callan moves to the other side just as Gordon brings out two small bowls of wide fried noodles — delicious with wonton, egg-drop, or matzo ball soup — and Mrs. Hocheiser (recognizing the real Gordon) accuses the nurse of fooling her. "You're not Gordon. Why'd you tell me you were Gordon?" Callan cautiously assures her, "I didn't. I never did."

The door to the kitchen is open, and Mother turns to see Gordon as he brings the tray of take-out to the table. "This is my son, you can't fool me; this is him." Mrs. Hocheiser now clutches Gordon's backside. Dishes rattle as the tray bumps the wall. Gordon tries holding it in balance, "Mom.... Mom."

Mrs. Hocheiser won't let go. "Ooooohhh, I'd know this tush anywhere. Is that a tush? There's never been a tush like it anywhere!" Gordon bends and wriggles to escape, "Ma, will you cut it out?" His mother now has freed his shirt from the back of his pants; his boxer shorts show. "What a tush." As Gordon pleads, "Ma, don't do this,"

Mrs. Hocheiser pulls his shorts down and kisses Gordon's naked tush with an affection traditionally reserved for the (other) soft cheeks of a baby.

Gevalt! Nurse Callan is astounded, aghast, and flabbergasted, and she flees the apartment.

Oedipal, shmoedipal, the man loves his mother!

Let me add another (for me and now for you) memorable link to this movie. I have just returned from the funeral of a kind and brilliantly witty friend. His name is Jim Gordon. That name is soundly associated with the movie: George Segal portrays Gordon Hocheiser; his mother is played by the actress Ruth Gordon.

And then there is this story:

One evening at a favorite Chinese restaurant in Little Silver, New Jersey, Jim took note that the paper placemats were decorated with Chinese representations of birth years — the year of the Horse, or Rat, or Tiger, or Rabbit, or Ox — and an embellished scrolling for the current year in the Chinese Calendar. "Do you see this?" Jim asked, indicating the ornamental font announcing the arriving Chinese New Year. "This is the year 4642 in the Chinese calendar! Do you know that it is the year 5766 in the Hebrew calendar?" I said I didn't know, but 5766 could be about right. "This means," totaled Jim, "that Jews went more than one thousand years without take-out!"

SLEEPER (1973)

"Like most of Allen's movies, this one is better than the box-office receipts would indicate; it still looks good many years after it was shot."
— *movies.tvguide.com*

"A comic epic that recalls the breathless pace and dizzy logic of the old two-reelers. Miles Monroe (Woody Allen), the part-owner of the Happy Carrot Health Food Restaurant in Greenwich Village, had gone into St. Vincent's Hospital in 1973 for a minor ulcer operation, only to wake up 200 years later, defrosted, having been wrapped in aluminum foil and frozen as hard as a South African lobster tail when the operation went somehow wrong."
— Vincent Canby, *New York Times*, December 18, 1973

"I had a wonderful time and I laughed all the way through, but [the movie] wasn't exhilarating. Allen's new sense of control over the medium and over his own material seems to level out the abrasive energy. You can be with it all the way, and yet it doesn't impose itself on your imagination — it dissolves when it's finished. If it sounds like a contradiction to say that [the film] is a small classic, and yet not exhilarating — well I can't completely explain that."

— Pauline Kael, *New Yorker*, December 31, 1973

Vincent Canby's synopsis and Pauline Kael's utter bafflement with the movie's perplexing paradox fits fine — even today. Many of the bits do fall into pieces of indisputable fun and wit, with obvious origin from the silent era; however, if not for the movie's sci-fi grounding, there would likely be no comprehensible whole.

The database's statement about Woody Allen's box office receipts vis-à-vis the quality of his craft brings to mind my memorable moment, an instance of such exceedingly constrained orientation that in a theater peopled by half the three hundred seats, only my wife and I laughed, and so uproariously that I'd have to believe the audience members — to this day — hold *our* mystifying reaction in *their* movie-going memory.

THE *SLEEPER* MOMENT: 0:11:36–0:12:31

The year is 2173, and under the watchful shelter of two scientists who released him from his cryogenic capsule into a fully defrosted and alert state following a medical mishap in a New York hospital in 1973, Miles Monroe (Woody Allen) is updated on the decisive events of the past two hundred years. He despairs that his rent is "two thousand months overdue!"

Miles asks about his friends, everyone else, and "Where am I anyhow?" And, when told, "You must understand that everyone you knew in the past has been dead nearly two hundred years," he pleads, "But they all ate organic rice." The briefing continues: "This is the Central Parallel of the American Federation. This district is what you probably called the southwestern United States. That was before it was destroyed by the war." Miles apprehensively inquires, "War?"

"Yes! According to history, over a hundred years ago, a man named Albert Shanker got a hold of a nuclear warhead!"

My wife and I roared with such an uncontrollable outburst that the audience turned from the screen to peer at us. Aware that the last line was lost to the rest of the house, and that however unintentionally, we had become a disruption, we did stifle ourselves with palms of both hands hard-pressed to our mouths.

We were wordless that in a five-college community (including the state university), no one else got it! Neither my wife nor I

— both born in 1940s New York — supposed that the moviegoers assembled that 1974 winter's day cared to hear the denotation of the Albert Shanker reference. Our mouths were hand sealed, and if a joke requires illumination, it's done for. And Woody Allen's humor needs a direct and instant snap to the gap between epic apprehensions and private anxieties.

If you've not laughed — or measured a chuckle — you'll welcome an explanation. If you were in attendance that day in Burlington, Vermont, I apologize for the distraction, and after these many years (before Google), I will detail the angst — and so too the awfully sinister hilarity — of Albert Shanker possessing a warhead.

In 1968, the New York State Legislature's plan for school decentralization — especially in minority communities — began an extended and divisive clash over school control and teachers' job security. At the center of the dispute was the Ocean Hill–Brownsville school district in Brooklyn, where many white teachers had been dismissed. Regrettably, the lasting anguish following the assassination of Dr. Martin Luther King Jr. contributed to the racial (and religious) hostility between school administrators, their parent supporters, and the teachers' union. Albert Shanker was president of the United Federation of Teachers, and in September he called a strike that closed 85% of New York City's 900 schools; as a result Shanker served fifteen days in jail. The discord intensified, and some community protesters threatened the lives of teachers and their families. Shanker's resolve made him an (undeserved) symbol of class and racial strife — if not warfare: in truth he was an active advocate of civil rights and worker's rights, but the flow of events warped all the adversaries into chaotic and fearsome absurdities.

Woody Allen's allusion supposed that the neighborhood "uproar" ended in nuclear destruction. There is an epilogue that engenders and refreshes my memory of the movie and the Vermont experience: Two decades later, I walked past Mr. Shanker along Third Avenue, between Twenty-Second and Twenty-Third streets, in New York City. He was bundled for the cold, attended by his wife, Edith; he looked incurably frail. Albert Shanker died of cancer in February 1997.

The memories and the research and writing lead me to deferential thoughts of the man.

DOG DAY AFTERNOON (1975)

"One of the finest films of the 1970s. Sonny (Pacino), to finance a sex-change operation for his transvestite lover (Sarandon), robs the First Savings Bank of Brooklyn with his moronic friend Sal. Police... surround the bank and hold the thieves inside."

— *movies.tvguide.com*

"Two men ineptly rob a Brooklyn bank that has only eleven hundred dollars in the vault. Though the farcical tone of the movie is blusterous, [it] succeeds, on the whole, because it has the crucial farcical virtue of not faltering. The achievement of a [style] note purely held very nearly carries the film through its flashes of crassness, though not altogether. There are some ill-earned laughs about homosexuals. Other sequences indulge in a sort of knowing psychoanalytic slapstick."

— Penelope Gilliatt, *New Yorker*, September 22, 1975

I find it surprising — if not shamefully alarming — that the movie was not selected for *The New York Times Guide to the Best 1,000 Movies Ever Made*. Outside the haphazard opening — structured with patchy footage — which is performed to a faux twangy (and tedious) Elton John song, the film still endures as one of the most imposing movies ever made.

Penelope Gilliatt's criticisms fault the familiar mid-twentieth-century expressions of a very long history of intolerance and phobias presumed by characters in the story with the values and thinking of the filmmakers, an oddly bungled observation. Certainly, the ineptitude of the robbers is not found in (nor a comment on) the skill of the production.

Director Sidney Lumet's accomplishment of containing a feature-length narrative to so few locations and so little time — effectively isolated to inside and (immediately) outside the First Brooklyn Bank for a period of hours — exceeds his master-of-craft presentation in *12 Angry Men*.

Sonny (Al Pacino) and Sal (John Cazale) are surrounded by (literally) bus loads of "New York's Finest," and a couple of FBI agents ready as well — at 0:34:38 there is a medium shot centered on two "suits": the man in front is Agent Sheldon, played by James Broderick, the father of Matthew.

THE *DOG DAY AFTERNOON* MOMENT: 0:32:37–0:36:04

In an attempt to negotiate the safe release of the bank employees, Detective Sergeant Moretti (Charles Durning) persuades Sonny — attended by a white handkerchief and a woman hostage (the head teller) — to step out and see how hopeless the situation is for the robbers. "Look up there. Look over here. Over here." Rooftops and sidewalks swarm with armed uniformed officers, many marksmen with rifles, and plainclothes detectives with guns drawn and aimed. The camera pans and tilts as Sonny's POV. There is unexpected calm; a surprising silence.

Sonny looks up and down and right and left. "You got the militia out here, huh?"

Moretti tries an appeal of incidental self-interest: "Quit while you're ahead. All you got is attempted robbery." Sonny, pacing the sidewalk, is alert: "Armed robbery!" Moretti does his best to remain unruffled. "All right, armed then. Nobody's been hurt. Release the hostages. Nobody's gonna worry over kidnapping charges. The most you're gonna get is five years. You'll be out in one year, huh?"

Nearly under his breath, Sonny mutters, "Kiss me, man." Moretti asks, "What?" Sonny continues becoming steadily more agitated: "Kiss me." He puckers and points to his lips. "When I'm being fucked I like to be kissed on the mouth."

Cuddled in the recess of the bank's front door is the woman teller. Sonny, as if a public defender, continues. "You're a city cop, right? Robbing a bank's a federal offense. They got me on kidnapping, armed robbery…. They're gonna bury me, man. I don't want to talk to somebody who's trying to con me. Get somebody in charge here."

Moretti calls out, "I am in charge here!"

Sonny, making intermittent eye contact, goes on. "I don't want to talk to some flunky pig trying to con me." Ignoring Moretti's efforts to keep the situation under control, he turns to his left, "What's he doing?" A cut contains Sonny — from over his right shoulder — and, to screen right, two helmeted officers in a group of others are taking aim.

Now, all hell almost breaks loose.

Sonny gestures with his hanky. "What are they moving in for?" Moretti scrambles into the police group and shoves one of the officers. "Will you get the fuck back there?! Get over there!"

Sonny takes command. "Go on back there, man. He wants to kill me so bad, he can taste it." Off-camera, we hear Moretti: "No one's gonna kill anybody."

Now, all hell *does* break loose: Sonny shouts "Attica" over and over and over, as he swaggers, waving his white handkerchief. Hundreds of spectators (a large crowd gathered and packed along police barricades) begin shouting and whooping and waving. Sonny adds, "Remember Attica?" and kicks the glass door to the bank. "Your word don't fuckin' matter." The entire neighborhood is now in chaos. Moretti shouts to be heard. "Come on. Come on. Calm down." Police officers hurry down the streets to assist in crowd control.

Sonny turns his attention back to the armed cops. "Put your guns down. If it wasn't for the TV guys, they'd kill us all." Moretti signals with arms waving downward. "Put your guns down; get back and put your guns down."

There is a single cut (medium shot) of Sal inside the bank. He holds his weapon at his chest and looks uneasily toward the street. The bedlam is beautifully muffled, making an abrupt contrast between inside and out, and so expanding the uproar. The crowd joins a unanimous chorus: "Put the guns down; put them down; put them down." Sonny skips along the sidewalk, his mouth in angry instigation, his hair blowing wildly. And then he again shouts, "Attica! Attica! Attica!" His handkerchief waves high to the rowdy onlookers. Back and forth he struts. "You got it, man. You got it, man. You got it, man." A helicopter's rotor-putting engine fades in, and a cut takes us high above the Brooklyn street; the camera (in an aerial shot) moves right, and a police helicopter appears and crosses the frame. Sonny is still shouting on the sidewalk below.

The events recorded in the movie actually occurred in August 1972, a year after a disastrous confrontation between state police and prisoners at an upstate correctional facility in Attica, New York. The inmates rioted — thirty-three correction officers were held hostage — in response to a prisoner's death at San Quentin the week before; but the mean-spirited conditions at Attica were motivation enough: inmates were allowed one shower per week and one roll of toilet paper per month. All the more than three hundred guards were white, while more than 50% of the prisoners were African American, and about 10% were Puerto Rican.

Negotiations were well under way, with several prominent journalists as attending witnesses, when Governor Nelson Rockefeller ordered an all-out assault. Thirty-nine prisoners and guards were killed.

Here, the movie, by way of its protagonist, plays on a long (and recent) history of anger and mistrust between law enforcement and diverse communities (especially minority) to rally favor and so claim a small victory — before a pathetic rout.

FANNY AND ALEXANDER (1983)

"A magical movie, [it] is likely to be the achievement for which Bergman will be most celebrated. [It] not only capture[s] the flavor and atmosphere of a Swedish town circa 1907, [it] expertly reveals events as seen through the eyes of a child."

— *movies.tvguide.com*

"Even as you watch Ingmar Bergman's new film, it has that quality of enchantment that usually attaches only to the best movies in retrospect, long after you've seen them, when they've been absorbed into the memory to seem sweeter, wiser, more magical than anything ever does in its own time."

— Vincent Canby, *New York Times*, June 17, 1983

"[In] what Bergman says is his final movie, his obsessions are turned into stories, and he tells them to us — he makes us a beribboned present of his Freudian-gothic dream world. [The film] is a festive and full-bodied dream play — a vision of family life as a gifted child might spin it around, turning himself into a hero, a magician, an actor. The picture is scaled big; it runs for three hours and ten minutes, and the glistening Christmas scenes, which go on for perhaps an hour, have a quality of fantasy and communal memory intertwined."

— Pauline Kael, *New Yorker*, June 13, 1983

The film, which was originally made for Swedish television in a week-long, five-hour presentation, won 1984 Academy Awards for Best Foreign Language Film, Best Cinematography, Best Art Direction, and Best Costume Design.

Ingmar Bergman has created "a vision of family life as a gifted child might spin it," a film doubtlessly not for a Saturday house matinee packed with youngsters, gifted or not; likely not even for contemporary adolescents, or at least not for their mindsets. Here is a fable for grown-ups — sincere and candid.

After a glorious Christmas Eve feast and the happiest of songs, the Ekdahl family, friends, and household staff wind their way in a hand-holding prance from room to room, singing, "Now it's Yule again, and Yule will last until it's Easter." The quick tempo leaves the aerobically challenged catching their breaths. The joyful frolic continues to tree decorating, which embraces sexual enticement.

A hefty man in a three-piece tuxedo with white bowtie topping a starched-stiff, shiny stud-beaded bib, gathers Fanny, Alexander, and their two young cousins — "Come children... come" — and promises, "Uncle Carl is going to treat you to one helluva fireworks show," then gestures the children onward. He follows carrying a lighted three-branch decorative candelabra and his cigar.

THE *FANNY AND ALEXANDER* MOMENT: 0:25:35–0:27:01

Inside a darkened marble-walled and stained-glass staircase, Uncle Carl hands the candelabra to a smiling Alexander. Intermittent clock bell-gongs chime Uncle, already with jacket off, down a short flight. Carl sniggers through his cigar-clasped mouth and, with grandiose flair, sits on the staircase's centered red carpet while concurrently unzipping his trousers.

As he removes his shoes, the children eagerly gather at the braidlike balustrade; their faces framed between railings, they giggle expectant approval to Uncle Carl, who lays his pants over the handrail and with a cigar salutation whispers, "Ready?"

Now, in tuxedo shirt, vest top, and long white underwear footed in black socks, Carl stands and slowly turns to upstairs. With an unpredictable and snappy tip backward he quick-step-scuttles up the stairs, then down and up again. This time, leaning low and forward, his face big in the film frame, he blows a blast of white smoke from his cigar and openly follows with a fart, which he pronounces "Number one."

The camera pans left to follow Uncle Carl's repeat (a petty, unforgivable pun) scurry down the steps. He grasps the banister's post to support a slight crouch — bracing as well against certain aeronautical-like laws of physics — and alerts, "Now comes number two." Carl's words are affirmed with a long drawn-out fart. The children are thrilled.

Uncle Carl slowly ascends the stairs while both his hands reach to the rear, and he unhurriedly unfastens the flap on his underwear. "Now comes number three."

As he reaches the landing — gulps of air confirm his hard slog — with rear flap down, he signals, "Bring the candles," and turns flap-side to the children; Alexander glides along the floor so that the lighted candelabra is sited at the level of Uncle's underside. The other children gather close and beam, eyeballing the exposed bottom. A short sharp burst blows all three holiday candles into darkness, with howls of children's fun.

This setting of childhood delights supplied by adult silliness — especially things daringly naughty and scatological — is cited in Pauline Kael's review: "It's a scene we usually get in a frat house movie." Yes! And I would say that is why context and creative sensibilities cannot be overvalued; but perhaps Vincent Canby's enchanted expression of absorbed movie memory is itself sweeter, wiser, and more magical than anything that needs saying.

FOLLY

It has been supposed, and so proposed, that what distinguishes humans from all other of nature's creatures is our use of tools. Believe it or not, I've witnessed, and more than once, mammals and birds employ tools. The instruments available looked nothing like a Stanley or Black & Decker mechanism, but I would think that the people accountable for species classification — primed for folly — would be hard-pressed to discriminate by upgrades in paraphernalia. The tools proviso has been shelved.

Later I learned that the ascribed trait was language. But in short order that proved inexact — if not untrue — save such a pigeonhole as vocabulary: that is, since it came to the attention of humankind that animals do communicate, and many with a distinct language, then our species might best be differentiated by the weight of our dictionaries. This may be a lawyerly loophole but a biologically scarce distinction.

Now there is a new genus defining conjecture: Humankind can, via memory, recall the past; be alert to the present; and imagine the future. I could agree, but the inference that we are so unaccompanied may not bear out.

The new hypothesis advises that animals grazing across Africa seem to return to relaxed eating soon after encountering a close call with a lion. This observation has led eager classifiers to conclude that zebras (for one) do not — and so cannot — imagine a life-threatening repeat in a future moment. Of course this suggests that zebras do not (cannot) recall their personal past; or that zebra brains do not (cannot) connect experience and imagination. In other words, they are constrained by instinctive immediate reactions.

I am no expert in this matter— did not major in such things at school — but many years ago, I raised chickens. With day-old chicks, I was instructed to place a shallow pan on the ground, fill it with the chicken grain, and peck a finger up and down into the feed. Silly as it seemed, I did it, and that single demonstration had the chicks on their way to egg-laying and roasts. The same sort of requirement was true for their shelter: they did not (would not) go into their outside ramped-door coop *until* I established that possibility, again with a single demonstration of placing each chick inside. From that moment on, at nightfall, they'd walk up the ramp.

But here's why I question the latest theory of human distinction: when on the first morning my chickens were grazing, and I came out of the house with a bucket of feed, they all panic-flapped away in a great cluck. I knew right away that they were responding to my very large, full-coated black Belgian sheepdog. I filled their eating pan, and as soon as Cappy and I headed for the house, the chickens hurried for the grain.

And here's my point: Starting the next morning and for every morning thereafter, the chickens rushed as if to greet me and my dog. They set aside their fear of the dog, having learned from one experience to remember that Cappy signaled that good grain was on the way.

The searching researches (almost) had a bird in the hand. What sets us apart is an uncontainable yearning to tell stories; and that attraction — across all movie genres — is often reflected in instances (small and large) of yet another distinguishing feature of our species: folly! Folly is the face at the ready, the imminent masquerade between comedy and tragedy.

By the way, I am resolute that zebras, in point of fact, have long reasoned — to use what must be their very own pet philosophy, "What else to do?"

THE BRIDGE ON THE RIVER KWAI (1957)

"This intelligent and exciting WWII tale, masterfully helmed by [Director David] Lean (at the start of his 'epic' period),... aptly juxtaposes action sequences with a psychological examination of the folly of war, emphasizing its many ironies (brought home most forcefully at the explosive finale)."
— *movies.tvguide.com*

"Brilliant is the word, and no other, to describe the quality of skills that have gone into the making of this picture, from the script out of a novel by the Frenchman Pierre Boulle, to direction, performance, photographing, editing, and application of a musical score. Alec Guinness does a

memorable — indeed, a classic — job in making the ramrod British colonel a profoundly ambiguous type. With a rigid, serene disposition he displays the tenacity of a lion, as well as the denseness and pomposity of a dangerously stupid, inbred snob. He shows, beneath the surface of a hero, the aspects of an inhuman fool. Here is a film we guarantee you'll not forget."
  — Bosley Crowther, *New York Times*, December 19, 1957

"The film is almost three hours in the telling, but there aren't many laggard moments. The picture is by no means the primitive account of the derring-do that we customarily find in movies about warriors; rather it's an adult blend of comedy, romance, satire, melodrama — and even after a cliff-hanging climax, a touch of tragedy."
  — John McCarten, *New Yorker*, December 28, 1957

The film is excusably thought to be the finest war movie ever made, likely because it is an "adult blend" of genres and worthy shades, not the least a tragedy, which springs from a psychologically dramatic prognosis of obsessive-compulsive disorder: more fittingly, Colonel Nicholson suffers obsessively, and compulsively, with *order*.

The glorious bridge awaits an approaching Japanese troop and supply train. Colonel Nicholson pompously passes one more inspection — footfalls parade the plankway, and he leans forward to secure trifling litter on the tracks. A pleased and relaxed look upriver is suddenly diverted down to the river, where the colonel detects wire just above the water line.

During the preceding night, a small British commando group had set the bridge with explosives controlled a short way downriver by Lieutenant Joyce, youngest commando, and sentinel of the detonator plunger. At daylight's arrival, a suddenly shallow river betrays the team's operation. An alarmed Joyce stealthily tosses handfuls of sand onto an exposed section of wire.

Colonel Nicholson considers the downriver side and views a dead tree branch sitting vertically out of the water. A wire is snagged on it. Nicholson advises the Japanese POW camp commander, Colonel Saito, "There's something odd going on."

THE BRIDGE ON THE RIVER KWAI MOMENT: 2:32:39–2:38:11

British Major Warden, the leader of the commando team, and American Navy Commander Shears, who, as an escapee of the Japanese prison camp, has directed the team to the bridge, watch from the opposite side of the river. In an extreme long shot (as POV), the branch, now in the foreground of the composition, resembles a periscope or the snout of a prehistoric snake, the snagged detonator wire producing an inverted "V" above the water line. The train's whistle — a piercing scream — and the ever-increasing level of the chugging-rumble of its engine spawn nervous expectation. Major Warden watches through binoculars as Nicholson follows the line and leads the Japanese commander progressively closer to Lieutenant Joyce, jeopardizing the commandos' plan: "He's gone mad. He's leading him right to it. Our own man!"

The river dips in a small fall — providing a more apparent streaming sound — ahead of Joyce's hiding place. A cawing of birds accompanies Joyce's POV of the approaching men. He pulls the plunger close and arms his automatic weapon. Nicholson stops with Saito behind him. Atop the gravely sand, out of the water's edge, gray cable is visible. Nicholson pulls at it, hand over hand, lifting it from the sand and into the distance. The cable stops, again snagged. Nicholson walks, pulling himself forward along the cable, pausing at a louder train whistle. A narrow gauge train moves toward the camera. Bleached white flags, with the intense red sun of Japan, criss-cross the engine front — a commemorative for the day.

Another long tug and the detonator wire yanks a flat rock employed to securely anchor the cable at the detonator. Joyce is hesitant to respond.

Shears pulls his knife, and as if certain of telepathic powers, pleads from across the river, "You've got to do it boy…. You've got to do it now!" Mind-bogglingly for Shears and audience alike, Joyce pulls *his* knife.

Nicholson asks Colonel Saito for a knife to cut the cable: "The bridge has been mined." As Saito reaches for his knife, Joyce charges from his hiding place, clasps a hand across Saito's mouth, and stabs him in the back. In partnership, Shears mimics the deed. Saito collapses into the water. Major Warden lowers his binoculars. "Good boy!"

Now Nicholson grapples with Joyce, holding his legs to keep him from the detonator, and the colonel bellows for help. Japanese soldiers hurry to the downriver side of the bridge. Warden scowls, "Kill him. Kill him." Shears soars to his feet, shouting with a wild wave of his right arm, "Kill him! Kill him!" Joyce pleads with Nicholson as he drags the colonel through the sand, getting closer to the detonator. "We're here to blow up the bridge…. Let me go, sir. You don't understand, sir."

Shears rushes down from his jungle cover and recklessly swims for the other side. The train whistle shrieks; Japanese rifle fire skips across the water, and a machine gun sprays the sand and strikes Lieutenant Joyce.

A firefight continues across the river: Major Warden launches mortar rounds as Nicholson, unexpectedly composed, roves to the river and the menacing Shears, who, mortally wounded, *crawls* to the shore. The wounding of Joyce and Shears strikes the women porters — or, as the film gives credit, "Siamese girls": Their reactions are all but pressed into my memory. Nicholson and Shears meet at the water's edge, and both utter "You." The colonel as inquiry, the returning POW with loathing.

Mortar shells continue across the river, landing among the Japanese soldiers. Nicholson stares at the detonator. "What have I done?" The train squeals louder as the colonel runs past the body of Joyce. A shell explodes, and he falls to the sand. Nicholson gets himself up, fetches his cap, dusting it across his pant leg. The chugging train engine is evident as Nicholson staggers ahead; the shrill whistle propels the train to a soft right curve and onto the bridge. In a heavenly stare, Nicholson's eyes roll back, and he slumps onto the plunger.

The bridge explodes and, in multiple angles, it and the train tumble into the river.

Ironically, the folly of war, represented in the screen adaptation penned by Carl Foreman and Michael Wilson, was wholly coordinated with the political folly of the Hollywood blacklist. It took nearly forty years before the Writer's Guild of America reinstated their screenwriting credit.

Or, as Major Clipton, in the movie's last words, observes, "Madness! Madness!"

VIRIDIANA (1961)

"Luis Buñuel had been absent from his native land for 25 years when he was invited by the Franco government to produce a film in Spain. Ironically, [the film] was never shown in Spanish theaters, having been banned by the government immediately after its debut at the Cannes Film Festival, where it won the Golden Palm. [The film] is filled with allegories concerning the general state of the world and Spain in particular, conveyed with the master surrealist's usual mix of black humor and stunning images."

— *movies.tvguide.com*

"[The film] came to the Paris yesterday. The theme is that well-intended charity can often be badly misplaced by innocent, pious people. Therefore, beware of charity. That is the obvious moral that forms in this grim and tumorous tale of a beautiful young religious novice who gets into an unholy mess when she gives up her holy calling to try to atone for a wrong she has done. But we strongly suspect that Señor Buñuel had more than this in mind when he made this intense and bitter picture."

— Bosley Crowther, *New York Times*, March 20, 1962

"Good fortune can be disconcerting — for the third week in a row, I've encountered a thoroughly admirable picture, and I find I must make an effort not to praise it too little simply because I've been praising other pictures so much. If it weren't for the fact that there are still plenty of third-rate Hollywood boffos being cranked out, which irritate me every bit as much as their predecessor did and thus serve to assure me that my critical faculties aren't turning to fudge. The pleasant truth of the matter is that movies may be entering a new golden age."

— Brendan Gill, *New Yorker*, March 24, 1962

"The Spanish film industry has been having a difficult time of it, plagued as it is by the limitations of censorship, and by cruelly restricted budgets. Nevertheless, a trickle of films have quietly slipped out of Spain and gained a great deal of attention for themselves on sheer merit. The most famous example is 'Viridiana,' the film made last year in Spain, at the invitation of the government, by Luis Buñuel, who had long since exiled himself to Mexico, but his enormous reputation tempted the government into trying to win him back. 'Viridiana' emerged — a wonderfully timed, savagely sacrilegious piece of observation, which he must have known would never pass the Censorship Office, and which he managed to smuggle out to Cannes in the luggage of a prominent bullfighter."

— Alastair Reid, Letter from Spain, *New Yorker*, September 29, 1962

The movie database provides an abridged account of the (historic) occasions that shaped the film; and though director Luis Buñuel's earlier film achievements — *Los olvidados* (1951) and *Él* (1952) — while an émigré from Spain during the Spanish Civil War (moving to the United States, then to Mexico [1946], where he became a citizen [1949]) received well-deserved critical praise, *Viridiana* earned him international notice. Buñuel's persuasive trick on Generalissimo Franco's dictatorship to get the film produced and smartly sneaked out of the country confidently proposed an agreement in distinguished folly!

The beggar's banquet scene, which featured Buñuel's replication of Leonardo di Vinci's *Last Supper* (the blind beggar placed as Jesus), may be the film's iconic memory; however, Viridiana's labors to supply a sanctuary and foodstuffs in bounty at the estate of her (deceased) uncle Don Jaime is monitored with equivalent folly by Jorge — the illegitimate son of the uncle — who disparages such benevolence. "It's stupid. Why care for twenty beggars when there are millions in the world."

Buñuel carries out a small "joke" that came to pass when the director was scouting locations. He noticed "especially in Alicante" (Spain), dogs walking behind carts, tied to the axle. The director made it clear, "Even though it [initially] didn't make much sense, like someone who puts a notation in the margin of a book... the episode did end up being integrated into the story."

THE *VIRIDIANA* MOMENT: 0:55:20–0:57:19

Don Jorge and an assistant are taking measurements of his land along a roadway. A cart passes with a dog tied to the axle. From behind Don Jorge, we watch (with him) as the mule-pulled cart rhythmically paces away. A head-on shot follows Jorge as he fixedly walks after the cart. The cart comes to a stop, and two soldiers climb out. The cart owner climbs off the back as well, and the soldiers thank him "for the lift."

As the cart man checks out the right wheel, Don Jorge arrives at his side. "Hey, this dog's exhausted. Why not let him ride in the cart?" The man explains, "The cart's only for people." Don Jorge proposes a compromise. "At least untie him. He'll follow you." But the cart man is also — if absurdly — protective of his dog, "What if he gets run over?" Don Jorge crouches, nearly going under the cart, and holds

the dog's face in both hands. "I'll buy him from you." The cart man stoops into the frame. "He's good at hunting rabbits. He knows he'll starve if he doesn't hunt." The tribute implies a point of bargain, but when Don Jorge asks, "How much?" the cart man answers, "Pay me whatever you like."

Don Jorge gets out his money. "Untie him."

Both men stand. Don Jorge hands the man some bills, and the man in turn hands over the dog. "Thanks and goodbye."

As the cart heads down the road, Jorge calls out, "What's his name?"
"Canelo."

Hearing his name, the dog tries to pull and go after his old master. Jorge holds the rope fast. "Easy boy. Come here, Canelo." The dog pulls again. A cut takes us to a master shot from behind Don Jorge, his assistant, and Canelo. The cart rolls on and away. Don Jorge bends to shorten the rope and pat the dog. "Easy, Canelo." He walks off to screen right.

Coming toward the camera on the opposite roadside — to screen left — is another cart; a man walks alongside, holding a short strap attached to the mule's bridal. We see that a dog is tied to the axle. In a medium shot we move along the road, ever so slightly behind the dog. Don Jorge does not see!

> "It is the abyss that can exist between an idea of the world and what the world really is. In fact almost all my characters suffer from a disillusionment and later change, for better or for worse."
>
> — Luis Buñuel

Brendan Gill's "good fortune" — and mine as well — at the time projected that "movies may be entering a new golden age." I think they were and did, but the 1960s were an inopportune time to hurry off to Blockbuster or online to Netflix to catch up on the work of any recently discovered directors.

I too got to see *Viridiana* at the Paris and straight away sought writings on, or by, Señor Buñuel; and I heeded each week's *Village Voice* for announced New York City appearances of any Buñuel film.

THE FRENCH CONNECTION (1971)

"A tough brilliant crime thriller. Young director [William] Friedkin produced a suspenseful and utterly absorbing film which incorporated thrills and street humor and routine police work with highly dramatic scenes."
— *movies.tvguide.com*

"[The film] opened yesterday at the Loews State 2 and Loews Orpheum. [It] is a film of almost incredible suspense, and it includes, among a great many chilling delights, the most brilliantly executed chase sequence I have ever seen. From moments very early on, you know that the world is cursed, and that everybody playing out his allotted role is cursed along with it."
— Roger Greenspun, *New York Times*, October 8, 1971

"And now an extraordinarily well-made new thriller gets the audience sky-high... [It] is one of the most 'New York' of all recent New York movies. The movie's suspense is magnified by the sheer pounding abrasiveness of its means; you don't have to be an artist or be original or ingenious to work on the raw nerves of an audience this way — you just have to be smart and brutal. This picture says that Popeye [Gene Hackman] is a brutal son of a bitch who gets the dirty job done. So is the picture."
— Pauline Kael, *New Yorker*, October 30, 1971

Pauline Kael's full review reminds me that incorrect memory is more intriguing than precise, because what is inaccurate helps initiate knowledge about the storerooms of memory and the complexities of their function. When we re-see and re-hear a movie moment — let alone re-smell, re-touch, or re-taste other re-collected instances — and realize that our memory is inaccurate, we are able to question how our brains accumulate (often with certainty) what did *not* occur. The answers can prove fascinatingly revealing, even if not neurologically, chemically, or psychologically diagnosable.

Kael writes, "How's this for openers? A *flic* strolls into a boulangerie, comes out carrying a long French bread, and strolls home. As he walks into his own entranceway, a waiting figure in a leather coat sticks out an arm with a .45 and shoots him in the face and then in the torso."

The "flic" is a Marseilles undercover detective — this is somehow unclear to Kael, though she uses the French for "cop." She writes later in her review, "And if you ever think about it, you'll realize that you have no idea who that poor devil was who got shot in the overture, or why." *Who*, by way of classic parallel editing, is soon linked to the goings-on with undercover cops in Brooklyn, New York.

The flic is ambushed in a hallway as he gets his mail from a line of tin boxes high on a wall. The killer fires a shot into the detective's face. There is no shot to the torso; there is but a *single* gunshot. Isn't this more wonderfully peculiar than being *unsure* about particulars, or having no memory of the scene at all? There are two shots (film cuts or clips, not gun blasts): one used to display the strike of the mortal head wound, the other the collapsing flic. Do the dual compositions, while the viewer is stunned by the moment, register as two gun shots? The assassin cruelly steals a heel of the fresh bread as he exits the hallway and abandons the remainder of the loaf, tossing it onto the *torso* of the dead flic. Does that alone, or in combination with the (two) cuts, attach in certain memory?

Notwithstanding the many brightly memorable moments — the Grand Central Shuttle scene; the commandeered car chasing the elevated train, "part of cinematic legend" and, as Greenspun corroborates, "the most brilliantly executed chase sequence I have ever seen"; or the tearing apart of the Lincoln Town Car at the police garage in search of the contraband heroin — I have selected a quintessential sequence of Popeye Doyle's compulsive-enforcement disorder, which proves the *Times*' reviewer's note of fateful folly: "The world is cursed, and... everybody playing out his allotted role is cursed along with it."

After the drug deal finally goes down on Wards Island (NYC), the boss, *the French connection*, Alain Charnier (known as Frog 1), snuggled inside the Lincoln with lots of cash, suddenly finds himself blocked by assembled police vehicles and detectives led by his relentless opponent, Popeye Doyle. Charnier's driver backs the vehicle into a spin and speedily returns to the island with the cops in high siren-wailing pursuit, setting off a noisy but run-of-the-mill shootout with the many crooks; Frog 1 flees into one of the grungy brick buildings — Doyle's determined quest has him close behind.

THE FRENCH CONNECTION MOMENT: 1:38:02–1:41:52

Doyle, with gun drawn, kicks open a cable-secured door gate, and the slamming sound reverberates over his POV: a long dark room of

decaying pillars and assorted sized windows. Odd broken objects are scattered along the floor. A tracking long shot moves with Doyle along a tile wall, in which dozens of square openings reveal mangled piping running vertically and horizontally — in appearance a long-ago abandoned factory, with lodging showers, lockers, and bathrooms. In reality, Wards Island served as an immigration post from 1860 until Ellis Island opened in 1892. The New York City Asylum for the Insane was located there in 1863; and the island became a reburial site for indigent souls (well over 100,000) formerly buried in Madison Square and Bryant Park graveyards. The site selected for the movie's end is ideal.

The easy and careful footfalls of Doyle are the only sound but for the location's dim ambiance. A simple strategy compels the cuts: Doyle on the hunt followed by his varied views.

Detective Mulderig walks the same path only seconds after Doyle, as outside, the shootout continues, the bad guys refusing to surrender. Eventually, well-aimed tear gas ends the battle.

The sound of dripping now joins the rummaging footsteps probing ever-wetter walkways of the plant. Doyle catches sight of a scampering figure, silhouetted against a backlit room, and he rushes forward, his face moving into close-up.

Doyle and the audience are simultaneously startled by a voice: "Popeye?" Doyle spins with gun (gripped with both hands) pointed straight out, both arms extended. It's Detective Russo. Doyle turns his attention to the distant area. Russo steps to his partner's right shoulder. Doyle concentrates ahead. "Frog 1 is in that room." This time the POV initiates a nervous compositional theme.

A strong cut back to the two detectives sets up their divergent paths and manner as they proceed to the room: Russo sensibly staggers his advance along the wall, alternating crouched forward progress with quick dips against whatever cover the scattered debris can provide, while Doyle marches upright for the room. The edits back and forth between the two detectives propose a tease via the contrast, and an apprehension of "cursed" fate.

Doyle's puff-out breaths are conspicuous in the chilled setting.

As the POV shots of "that room" become larger, closer, Doyle hears a sound to his right; he turns his head, and seeing a shadowy figure, he raises his gun, calling, "Drop it!" and fires off shots enough to empty his revolver in ricocheting blasts that crumble plaster to a tumbling mess. Russo plummets backward against the wall, hands and arms covering his head; then he, ahead of Doyle, rushes the fallen shadow.

A close-up discloses Detective Mulderig, eyes open and nearly crossed, his head so steadfastly pinned to the wall that his hat — still atop his head — is crunched and tilted, giving the dead detective the look of a disheveled drunkard.

Dumbfounded, Russo utters, "Mulderig. You shot Mulderig!"

Doyle is already reloading his gun. "The son of a bitch is here. I saw him…. I'm going to get him!" With severe breaths, he clicks shut the cylinder and restarts his hunt, now backtracking the long halls of Wards Island. To Doyle, Detective Mulderig's death is simply predictable collateral damage.

A moaning tone builds into the score as Doyle quickens his steps into the background; he gets ever smaller until a slight right has him disappear from view. A single shot rings out. The moment could imply that our protagonist — dishonored or feeling guilty — has taken his own life, but not Popeye; we would more correctly assume that his dogged pursuit of Frog 1 continues, or that he's shot another wrong guy.

The film truly is so remarkably "absorbing" that it captivates the viewer with the most "routine [of] police work." Though the vast majority of the movie plays in superfluous stakeouts and tailings and chasings — in cars and on foot — Friedkin and company have constructed a superb thriller.

COLONEL REDL (1985)

"This is an expertly made historical drama that, while fictionalizing some events, truthfully examines the desire for power and the catalysts of war…. A tour de force performance by [Klaus Maria] Brandauer as Colonel Alfred Redl, who became head of the Austro-Hungarian military intelligence bureau in the early 1900s, despite his impoverished origins. The film won the Jury Prize at the Cannes Film Festival and received an Oscar nomination for Best Foreign Film."

— *movies.tvguide.com*

The film was a Golden Globe nominee for Best Foreign Film, an Academy Award nominee for Best Foreign Language Film, and the winner of the British Academy Award for Best Foreign Language Film and the 1985 Cannes Film Festival Jury Prize, yet it does not appear in *The New York Times Guide to the Best 1,000 Movies Ever Made*, nor in *The Complete New Yorker* DVD set.

The film is inspired by the John Osborne play *A Patriot for Me* and followed director István Szabó's collaboration with actor Klaus Maria Brandauer on *Mephisto*, the 1981 Academy Award winner for Best Foreign Language Film.

Perhaps the Folly label could signal the silliness of the selection processes by which films are assigned for review or archived and categorized for history (memory). The label might well describe the foolishness of military and political machinations — a central ingredient in the film's plotting — but I position the work here because of a delusion held by my mother's Galicia (Poland) family and advanced to me when I was a boy, a delusion I would remember with an immediate ironic laugh upon viewing the movie as an adult.

One Thursday evening, *Colonel Redl* came into view by brief chance as I walked along Monmouth Street in Red Bank, New Jersey. I was on my way home from the train station when I caught sight of the small neighborhood movie house across the parking lot from Bilow's Liquors. As soon as I stepped in the door, I telephoned the theater for the scheduled showings. As it turned out, the movie was playing that evening alone, and the next — and last — showing started in about thirty minutes. My wife and I expected a sell-out crowd for sure, so we rushed down White Street to buy our tickets. There were no other customers outside the theater; there were none inside either — my wife and I had complete choosing rights to every seat in the small house.

With less than five minutes to show time, and hardly into the previews, the double side doors toward the back opened and a pageant of the elderly — and older — marched in to take their seats. Many were held and balanced on canes and walkers; a few carefully assisted their most wobbly friends. "Here," I thought, "are local survivors of the Austro-Hungarian Empire."

The masterful movie might well be memorable for creative quality alone, or for its exaggerated chroma choices — an overall bluish hue for daylight, and orange for artificial. These provide easy recommendation from me to others, but there is also the moment that set off the immediate ironic laugh.

The film's head credits, in glowing red titles, play in company to an assertively upbeat march by Strauss and across intermittent cuts of Redl's portrait, the stills at times alive though static, and what is soon disclosed to be images occurring in memory: Alfred (Redl) as a young boy.

There is his father as saluting policeman; or is he a station master? Next is his mother at a well, and sisters and shepherd dog chasing and playing. Family members in clear eye contact continue to acknowledge the camera at "wash-up" and dinner and bedtime. Alfred's beloved mother extinguishes a lamp light with a gentle breath, leans forward with a satisfying "goodnight" smile, and slowly moving away, she blows out the oil lamp lighting her side of an overly ornate, dark boarded bed. An oval portrait hangs in a flamboyantly centered square frame above the bed. A cut brings a close-up of the photo: a proud mustached man in a military jacket, his hair cropped but for a curl-centered wave. Alfred's mother's voice narrates the briefest of Redl family history.

THE *COLONEL REDL* MOMENT: 0:03:23–0:03:33

"Your grandfather was a friend of his majesty the kaiser. The kaiser once asked him, 'Well, my friend, what's new?'"

The two sentences do not make for a joke, yet I laughed aloud, and the old moviegoers turned to have a look at me. My mother, born of peasant Polish Jews, orphaned of both parents by age four — suffering the eternal anxiousness of such fate — had tucked me into bed one night thirty-eight years earlier and, pressing the first two fingers of her right hand together, conceitedly announced, "Your grandfather and the kaiser were like this!"

My mother's gesture served as an oath of loyalty to a vanished kingly acquaintance, offering a tad of significance to remarkably common stock, desperately, sadly, but so very dearly, delusional. I think my uncontainable movie-house laugh was a swift challenge to unshakable feudal spirits, my mother's birthright.

No one else in the audience laughed: All were likely members of the aristocracy, or royal family ancestors of the Hapsburg's long reign between the thirteenth and twentieth centuries in Europe, a reign that included the Holy Roman Empire, Spain, and Austro-Hungary.

The face in the film's framed portrait is quite like that of the young Emperor Franz Joseph, though the tunic is less than royal, and the image would have had to have been captured at the threshold of photography. The only portraits that I could find of Franz Joseph at that age are painted, and he is costumed in richly regal wear. And if, as implied by Redl's mother, it is a photograph of his grandfather, I wonder about the comfort in consummating a marriage under parental eyes: a happenstance of Sigmund Freud's association to psychoanalysis and the empire?

When the film ended and the exiting slowed in wait for so many walkers and canes, I caught a glimpse of a white bus at curbside, the driver ready to assist his passengers. I could swear the black letters along the full length of the bus read "House of Hapsburg Assisted Living Center."

But I won't.

[Cinema is] an art medium whose potentials are continuously beyond the reach of its practitioners.

— *Roger Angell*

EPOCH

The Roger Angell comment that precedes this chapter is from his excerpted review of *Breathless*, the first entry in the Epoch category. The insight of the quote in specific context inspired a modest amendment. Angell brings an astonishing perspective on preceding filmmaking epochs and prospects in the offing. I might have altered his words to a provocation and a dare. I think that good and right!

"I think [some] of those historically important films haven't worn well because their innovations have become commonplace — too successful in a sense — while there isn't enough in them to engage our interest today."
— Dwight Macdonald

"It isn't easy to come to terms with what one enjoys in films, and if an older generation was persuaded to dismiss trash, now a younger generation, with the press and schools in hot pursuit, has begun to talk about trash as if it were really very serious art."
— Pauline Kael, "Trash, Art, and the Movies," *Harper's*, February 1969

In an epic sense, I have spent few years on earth. I have rounded the sun a meager sixty-eight times. By the basics of the world's moviemaking era, I have been hanging around for well over half. Let me spotlight some films that were of a mind with their time (my time too) and that in turn projected a forecast.

BREATHLESS (1960)

"What Stravinsky's 'Le Sacre du Printemps' is to 20th-century music or Joyce's *Ulysses* is to the 20th-century novel, Godard's first feature is to film. It stands apart from all that came before and has revolutionized all that followed."

— *movies.tvguide.com*

"New-wave French films have aroused moral concern and have received criticism. It started two years ago (then called 'les films des jeunes') by young directors with new camera eyes and a shoestring to work on. They used decors that cost nothing, sidewalk cafes, and beds. One of these films 'Á Bout de Souffle' — directed by Jean-Luc Godard — is the best French film of any kind this year."

— Janet Flanner, Letter from Paris, *New Yorker*, August 13, 1960

"As sordid as is 'Á Bout de Souffle,' which came to the Fine Arts yesterday — and sordid is really a mild word for its pile-up of gross indecencies — it is withal a fascinating communication of the savage ways and moods of some of [today's] rootless young people. [The film] progresses in a style of disconnected cutting that might be described as pictorial cacophony. Say this, in sum [the film] is certainly no cliché. It is more a chunk of raw drama, graphically and artfully torn with appropriately ragged edges out of the tough underbelly of modern metropolitan life."

— Bosley Crowther, *New York Times*, February 8, 1961

"In an art medium whose potentials appear to be almost continuously beyond the reach of its practitioners, a master work is likely to be handicapped by excessive praise. Since there is no help for this that I can see, I must risk injuring a French film called 'Breathless' (created by the New Wave director Jean-Luc Godard) by saying quickly that it is far and away the most brilliant, the most intelligent, and most exciting movie I have encountered this season. M. Godard and his associates make comprehensible, and therefore touching and serious, the lives of two disorderly, disconnected, nihilistic young moderns. I am confident that it will be imitated endlessly, and probably ineptly, by dozens of film-makers, and that it may even threaten the Kennedys as the warmest topic of local conversation for weeks to come."

— Roger Angell, *New Yorker*, February 11, 1961

The *TV Guide* movie database assigns too much influence — and so, a burden — to the impact of any single work. It ignores convention and the rules that erect defensive agendas of an era, confining forces of creativity till someone or something exposes such foolishness, seeing that there are no rules — not really — only imagined (and feared) parameters of refuge and chariness that are eventually stirred or shoved to new "unlimited" boundaries.

No one need deny that Jean-Luc Godard stretched film grammar, yet the foremost realization may be *Breathless'* tripodless photography of locations and characters of daring impulsiveness: Godard convinced critic and public that cinema welcomes vast possibilities.

The movie arrived in New York City more than a year after its homeland release, and I rushed to see it. Though the disjointed "pictorial cacophony" earned it much of its standing, its inescapable disparities with the big studio films of the time — it was not in dazzling Technicolor, and it "aroused moral concern" — proved to be far more crucial to me.

I cherished the film for an intuitive bond let loose by its emergence at the time of my budding adulthood, mostly marked in serene steps toward rebellion: I read beat generation writers; I read the Jean-Paul Sartre trilogy and learned the correct and forceful throat-clearing pronunciation of his name; I attended an early performance at The Circle in the Square of Jean Genet's *The Balcony*; I ignored barber shops, letting my hair down (to my shoulders) and was far more sexually earnest with women.

Photographed in unembellished black and white, emphasizing characters and places similarly unadorned, the work supplied "brilliant" and "exciting" filmmaking; the "sordid" was a "fascinating communication of the savage ways and moods of some of the rootless young people."

My many screenings over these past fifty years never exclude the initial allure of the movie's flair, of actor Jean-Paul Belmondo, and of the main character Michel's interest in American actor Humphrey Bogart. I was, at first viewing, astonished by the achievement of many of the boldly presented moments; I was, at other times, unpredictably — what with limited experience or thinking about such matters — alert to the film's lapses: too dedicated to a technique that, on occasion, overwhelmed the moments of the story. Yet, the film's inventive risks of failure carry on and are worth applauding.

The *Breathless* Moment: 0:01:56–0:05:31

The film's protagonist — and attendant societal antagonist — Michel drives a country road in a jump-started stolen sedan. He is charming, engaging, and, while not handsome, undeniably attractive. He sings of love and, with eyes to the camera, engages the audience: "If you don't like the sea, if you don't like the mountains, if you don't like the city, then get stuffed!"

He complains about maddening drivers and traffic jams and the looks of hitchhiking young women. He finds a pistol in the glove compartment and play-shoots at passing motorists and at the sun sparkling in the fleeting leaves of roadside trees. Michel's pretend firing, "pow-pow-pow," leads to imaginary (though actual) gun blasts. His speeding gets the attention of two motorcycle officers: "Shit, the cops!"

A series of hurried glimpses of autos and echoes of engine revs cuts to a view out the back window of the sedan; this instantly jumps to a closer-fitting shot that, in a snap, eliminates the truck the police were (an instant ago) approaching. A very rapid yet uncompleted pan right; a cut of the sedan flying down the wrong side of the road; a single horn beep, and the motorcycles flying across the screen, though now right to left — the opposite direction at this moment in the chase — carries Michel's stolen auto to a dirt path only yards from the highway.

Michel complains, "The jump lead's gone," as he leans out the passenger window clasping his cigarette. Quickly, there is a single motorcycle officer passing the entranceway to the dirt path, and a cut back to the sedan shows Michel now suddenly outside the front of the vehicle, opening the hood. "What stinking luck." Another cut, and the second motorcycle officer rides by. Michel is now twist-joining electric wires; he hears a motorcycle engine and looks up. An easy POV shows that one of the motorcycle officers has found Michel's dirt path, and as the bike screeches to a stop, Michel hurriedly leans into the passenger window of the car.

While a fractured string of shots undoubtedly "state" that Michel shoots and kills the cop, they may be the most disjointedly bemused and cadenced cuts in movie history: The phrase "Stop or I'll kill you" barely precedes a strange tilt down to a close-up of Michel in profile. He is now looking to screen right, though the cop was arriving to the

left. It is oddly vague as to whether the voice of the threat is that of Michel or the officer, though the scene visually implies it is the motorcycle cop's warning. The image that precedes the tilt down is of Michel's back as he is reaching into the car, and there is a brief recognition of a shadow cast upon his shirt. The tilt downward does, of course, pass Michel's ear — are the officer's words arriving? The tilt no sooner arrives at Michel's white shirt then it cuts and pans right along his rolled-up sleeve, to his bracelet and hand holding the pistol. We spot the thumb pull down on the hammer. A "click" cuts to an extreme close-up of the gun's cylinder rolling downward, and the pan continues rightward along the full length of the barrel.

A gunshot rings out, and a more commonplace composition shows the police officer — the contrast between his medium-value uniform and bright white belts and gloves assists in the clarity — toppling into a wooded area. A panning master shot follows Michel running across a field, his black tie blowing across his left shoulder, cued to peculiarly histrionic music.

Often, along with the very "latest" methods come those of earlier eras: *Breathless* makes use of the silent movie device of an iris close to focus the audience on two detectives "looking" for Michel, and an iris open as a transition to the next scene; and the music is a "cacophony" of (at times) over-the-top 1950s TV series scores.

In my sociology class at college, Albert Camus' novel *The Stranger* was required reading. The lecture and discussions provided intellectual explanation of the book and its author's place in existentialism. Jean-Luc Godard's *Breathless* granted emotional appreciation of the nineteenth-century philosophy and its more radical and politically upsetting notions of the mid-twentieth century. Most vital of all, the film persuaded me to a career path that I continue to treasure and a conviction that filmmakers can indeed produce art.

LAST YEAR AT MARIENBAD (1961)

"The cinematic equivalent of the *nouveau roman* ('new novel') and a true landmark in film history. One of the most formally inventive of all feature films, *Last Year at Marienbad* stretches the limits of film language to the extreme."

— *movies.tvguide.com*

"The French film arrives here already famous for having stirred violent feelings pro and con in Paris and London, and local pride would seem to require that we in New York respond to it with equal violence, but for once my gift for chauvinism fails me; I simply and uncombatively like the picture very much.... [It] flows past one's eyes with the suavity and the never-to-be-questioned illogic of a dream, and indeed it may be that we are intended to perceive that its story is a sort of dream within a dream.... [A] young woman appears to be married; [another] man wishes her to run away with him and assures her that he became her lover a year ago, at Marienbad, and that she had begged him to allow her one more year of her accustomed life. At first the woman claims to remember nothing about Marienbad, but the man is strong and sure of himself; we sense that she is breaking down and that whether she had actually been at Marienbad is less important than his being able to convince her that she had been."

— Brendan Gill, *New Yorker*, March 10, 1962

Writing about a film released shortly after *Breathless*, and after decades of — I'd expect — deliberation, the database team is again unhinged. This may be what comes with excessive viewing of merely mainstream fare.

Brendan Gill's frankness from a half century ago upholds my confidence in communal facility and civility: Despite "violent feelings" aroused by the film's atypical time configurations or discernments in realities — expectations of established (time-honored) truths in story premise — the critic allocates a "flow" of "suavity" and dream illogic, an occurrence that was actually planting cinema "back" on its roots.

Resnais' manner, for film and art, whirls onward. Inquiry reveals a documentarian's heart: *Toute la mémoire du monde* (1956), a peerless enterprise for the French National Library (Bibliothèque nationale), centered on the archiving of history: "Because he has a short memory, man amasses countless memory aids."

The score and moving camera choreographed for *Toute la mémoire du monde* implement a divine sensuality also bared in *Hiroshima Mon*

Amour and *Last Year at Marienbad* — the films are interrogations into gathered memories.

My attempts to follow lines of analysis fetched a bounty of dips and peeks, here and there, and rounded out lots of reminiscences: "mon amour" so easily floated up, as if an episode of only yesterday — or "last year."

Two French soldiers, who had fled tank service in Algeria for the coffeehouses of Greenwich Village, hosted my initiation into Gitanes ("gypsy women") and Gaulloise cigarettes at the Fat Black Pussycat on Minetta Lane. They, along with others, were spending single-minded afternoons and evenings, and sometimes afternoons into late nights, playing a peculiar puzzle game using wooden matches. The game, as it turned out, was called nim and, as far as I could tell, was known to all the regular hangers-out at the coffeehouse through the release of Resnais' second feature film.

I was, at this time, one (small) part of the New York Poets Theater Company, an avant-garde assembly of dancers, actors, photographers, and playwrights at the Off-Bowery Theatre on East Tenth Street, a neighborhood later named — by realtors with too much self-esteem and renters with far too little — the East Village. The wild mingle of this Off-Off-Broadway house included, absent any order, Diane di Prima, Yvonne Rainer, Freddie Herko, James Waring, Alan Marlowe, LeRoi Jones (later Amiri Baraka), Michael McClure, Jack Smith, Louis Walden, Penny Ross, Deane Selmier, and me.

One evening, a (more than) beautiful girlfriend of Deane Selmier's attended the company's John Cage and James Waring one-act plays. I was cast in both that season and innocent of the girlfriend's attendance. A few days later, this dazzling redhead spotted me at the Fat Black Pussycat, sitting with the ever-present white mug of coffee and my friend Jeff, whom I knew as a hopeful photographer — a while later, when he was arrested in possession of fine art and museum antiquities, I learned that he was already an accomplished master thief. Betsy Bone — that was her name — recognized Jeff as a past date of one of her friends, and under this cover of acquaintance, she settled at our table. By evening's end, Betsy and I shook hands, and in that week, we made first-date plans to go see a movie: Alain Resnais' was playing at the Carnegie Hall Cinema on Fifty-Sixth Street and Seventh Avenue.

Betsy, appearing in high-spike heels and a woven bespoke coat of nubbles, and I took the subway uptown. I wore, far too ironically, a recently acquired navy blue trench coat, which had been charted for discard by Uncle Yankel and, if it had been rightly tailored to me, would have provided cloth enough for another.

A line of moviegoers was long and a fair distance from the box office. We took our place, but when, at last, we arrived at the ticket seller's window, she announced that the show was sold out. We purchased tickets (which were accompanied by a pamphlet with a synopsis to soothe audience confusion or anger — all told, an appeal to nonviolence) for the next and last nightly showing and walked over to Central Park, where we sat on one of the first benches from the street. Here was an occasion to inform, and we took turns offering a history of our lives. On that evening we could not recognize, lacking the experience, that we were closer to toddlers in time than to full-fledged folks: I was a month into being twenty, and Miss Bone was closing in on eighteen.

I learned that Betsy had met Deane Selmier during the previous summer when she joined the student company of the Shakespeare Festival at Stratford, Connecticut, and that she was in her senior year of high school. I do not recall anything that I reported.

Luckily, we started back for the cinema with time to spare because Betsy lost one of her long heels to a wide sidewalk seam and then slowly made her way, on my arm, in the saunter of someone with a severe leg-length discrepancy. Unfortunately, wobbling en route, eye shadow started seeping down her right cheek, a result of a contact lens paining that eye. She required the movie house's ladies room, and as I waited in the lobby, the new — and equally long — line of ticket holders filed in and filled the auditorium so that when we sought seats, pairs were no longer available. We sat dozens of rows and two aisles apart.

And so, despite the alluring glamour and sensual mystique illumined on the screen, my romantic fervor went weedy, and I came to recall one moment alone: the infectious and irresistible game of nim.

The game was demonstrated and explained at 0:16:15, using sixteen cards arranged in a four-row pyramid of seven, then five, then three, and one. Each of the two players, taking turns, removes as many or as few cards as desired, but they must be selected from only one of the rows per turn. The player left with (or picking up) the last card is the loser. The "Escort/Husband" won that round against the "Stranger," advising before the start of the game that "I never lose." The Stranger declared, "If you can't lose, that's no game." "I can lose," was the reply, "but I always win."

THE *LAST YEAR AT MARIENBAD* MOMENT: 0:22:44–0:24:42

Here now was the challenge, using (the Fat Black Pussycat-familiar) wooden matchsticks: The Stranger watches the Escort/Husband play against a hotel guest. The Escort/Husband — just as he forecast — wins. "Impossible," says the parting loser. The Stranger replaces the guest at the game table so that he is seated opposite the standing Escort/Husband and arranges the matchsticks himself. "What if you go first?" The Escort/Husband does and, in the end, the Stranger is left the last match.

Highlighting that evening's inclusive memory is the movie scenario's bond with the three off-screen characters: I entered the picture as the Stranger, but in the end, Deane Selmier was far stranger than I. Elizabeth Ann Bone married me in August 1962. We are still together, and both much closer to adulthood.

For the life of me, I cannot remember the trick promising a nim win every time!

In May 2009, director Alain Resnais presented a new movie, *Wild Grass*, at the Cannes Film Festival. He received a lifetime achievement award for a long, distinguished, and influential career. He was eighty-seven years old.

BONNIE AND CLYDE (1967)

"[A] landmark gangster film that made a huge commercial and cultural splash as it reimagined the two rural Depression-era outlaws as largely sympathetic nonconformists. The film set new standards for screen violence, but it alternated its scenes of mayhem with lyrical interludes and jaunty slapstick sequences accompanied by spirited banjo music. While unusual for a Hollywood feature, such jarring shifts in tone were typical of the genre-bending works of the French New Wave directors François Truffaut and Jean-Luc Godard, both of whom were slated to direct the feature at various points in its genesis."
— *movies.tvguide.com*

"Americans have a long tradition of celebrating our antiheroes. Rarely have we embraced as rancid a pair of ne'er-do-wells as the bumbling Depression-era stickup artist Clyde Barrow and his girlfriend Bonnie Parker. Finally tracked down and killed on May 23, 1934, they remained all but forgotten, relegated to pulp magazines and a B movie or two, for 30 years. The infamy they enjoy today can be traced almost exclusively to the wonderfully filmed, if thematically wrongheaded, 1967 movie, a paean to hippie-era themes of anti-authoritarianism and youth rebellion."
— Bryan Burrough, *New York Times Book Review*, May 10, 2009

"This blending of farce with brutal killing is as pointless as it is lacking in taste, since it makes no valid commentary upon the already travestied truth. It is loaded with farcical hold-ups, screaming chases in stolen getaway cars that have the antique appearance and speeded-up movement of the clumsy vehicles of the Keystone Kops."
— Bosley Crowther, *New York Times*, April 14, 1967

The film did not "re-imagine," it *imagined* the two rural Depression-era outlaws as "largely sympathetic nonconformists." While some folks might have considered the two "sympathetic," I don't know that Depression-era citizens characterized killer-robbers as "nonconformists." But, given the 1929 crash of the stock market and the ensuing dislike of banks and Wall Street, there likely was a measurable increase in fantastic imaginings of law-breaking to (pretend to) get back at the bastards, a sort of safe, yet satisfying, "getting even" effect of anger and frustration. Isn't that a more robust response to economic and social calamity than current Teabagger or Birther-parading pageants? At the very least, fancying oneself an outlaw concentrates the brain.

According to the movie database — and I have no cause to doubt — the film might have been assigned to one of the eminent directors of the French New Wave, information that, as intrigue alone, sets another correlation to Epoch. Tagging the movie's screen violence as setting "new standards" implies a requisite pat on the back — with contemporary works by Scorsese and Tarantino sharing commercial success, maybe deservedly so. Crowther's observation about the blending of farce and brutal killing is, for the most part, what set the film apart, and why wouldn't that indicate a pointless lack of taste?

I do think that the appeal of *Bonnie and Clyde* has much to do with casting — Faye Dunaway and Warren Beatty — that outperformed the contentious "imaginings" of the true-to-life subjects and the movie's "new standards of violence"; endearingly pretty people can easily encourage a setting aside of moral implications, if not merely adherence to law.

Much of the movie's newness, innovation, and rule breaking turns out to be a wholehearted revisiting of European (Russian) montage: a story revealing and (oddly) *sensitive* musing for a juxtaposition of images; in other words, a return to the ideals of cinema.

Clyde and Bonnie (who are, of course, essentially Warren and Faye) leave town, one step ahead of the Sheriff's Department and minus gang member C. W. Moss, whose "Pa" Malcolm has made a pact with law enforcement to entrap the two in return for "going easy" on his son.

C. W. Moss, following his pa's caution, stays put in the hardware store after Clyde and Bonnie finish grocery shopping, and a couple of deputies drive up and park alongside the robbers' handsome beige (stolen) touring car.

Not only are the two without C. W., but Clyde — at the wheel — is minus one lens of his sunglasses: an opaque lens hides his right eye, while his left sits circled by frame alone. Bonnie reaches into the grocery bag on the back seat and, in sumptuous succor, she shares a good-looking green pear with Clyde: The allusion to a (nearly) blind send-off from Eden may well be too brazen.

THE *BONNIE AND CLYDE* MOMENT: 1:47:43–1:49:00

Malcolm has feigned tire trouble along the country road that Clyde and Bonnie will be taking when they leave town. As the touring car approaches, Malcolm beams with both arms high in the air — an open hint to "stick-em up"? His gestures make clear there's trouble, and Clyde pulls off the road and alongside Malcolm's truck.

Bonnie waits in the car. Clyde exits, leaving the driver's side door open, and sees to lending Malcolm a hand. Clyde seems stress-free, the almost fully munched pear in his hand, and half his white shirt fluttered over his left pant leg.

Malcolm spells things out. "Got a flat tire. Ain't got no spare."

An almost-smiling Bonnie watches, and Clyde in profile gently chews the pear bits in his mouth. Malcolm spots a truck coming down the road: This sets off a series of quick cuts that, were it not for the rate, would classically assemble the about-to-spring ambush:

Malcolm, with a look of apprehension, looks to his left / Clyde, unconcerned, does too.

Quail flap abruptly from the trees / Clyde's face continues to his left, watching the flight with delight / Malcolm's eyes follow the birds / The quail are now over the tree line, into the sky / Bonnie watches in amazement / Two quail fly into the refracted light of sun on the camera's lens / Malcolm shifts his focus downward / A brambly thicket fills the frame / Malcolm regards his next move as his eyes shift again / The truck is fast approaching / Malcolm dives under *his* truck / Clyde turns (a very swift cut) to see Malcolm / Bonnie — rather relaxed — looks toward Malcolm / Malcolm edges farther under his vehicle / Clyde, looking downward, smiles, "Hey," then turns to look to his left; his expression is transformed to immediate misgivings / Bonnie too is startled and she looks to her left / The brambly thicket fills the frame / Bonnie instantly looks back to Clyde / Clyde dips in a fearful crouch / Bonnie, her face filling the screen, looks longingly to Clyde / A snap-fast cut back to Clyde / Bonnie's face, still full screen, slightly tilts left / Clyde moves to screen right, nearly leaving the frame.

Gunfire now erupts from the thicket. Branches and leaves are shredded.

The overkilling is so excessive, certainly in hindsight, that it nearly creates a foolish spoof on the cowboy-movie joking-game of shooting a six-shooter — maybe two — at the ground and right on up to someone's feet, ordering them to dance: Bonnie and Clyde in terrible twitching gyrations without melodic or dramatic rhythm.

EASY RIDER (1969)

"A must-see, if only once. Most notable as a document of its times than as a piece of cinema. [The film] is slack but powerful, sentimental, yet scathing, experimental but predictable.... Insufficiently developed as a satire of middle America, [it] seemed the paragon of hip rebellion at the time of its release; in retrospect, its worldview seems closer to whining self-pity."
— *movies.tvguide.com*

"[The movie], which opened yesterday at the Beekman, is a motorcycle drama with decidedly superior airs about it. As written and played [bikers Wyatt and Billy] are lumps of gentle clay, vacuous, romantic symbols, dressed in cycle drag. [The film,] directed by Dennis Hopper, won a special prize at this year's Cannes festival as the best picture by a new director (there was only one other picture competing in that category)."
— Vincent Canby, *New York Times*, July 15, 1969

"[The movie] is constructed like a ballad with a recurring fourth line. Between the verses describing the heroes' hardening encounters with America, there are repeated camp-fire scenes and mute cycle-riding sequences overlaid with pop music. Millions of words have been written explaining every element in this film's substance — hippies, idle violence; American restlessness; the reviving thing about the picture is that it doesn't explain, it embodies. The cant of cool is here made eloquent."
— Penelope Gilliatt, *New Yorker*, July 19, 1969

The database too hastily rejects a re-look. The film is considerable as an expression of the collective disorder during the civil rights–Vietnam era, and it is surprisingly unconstrained by "its times." It posits the onset of a prolonged and fierce adversarial divide — consider the past three presidential elections, health care reform, and gay rights — across regional (if not "tribal") America.

Penelope Gilliat's "doesn't explain, it embodies" casts a central measure of successful filmmaking: showing or demonstrating rather than verbal exposition and explanation. It may be that a rule-breaking breakthrough is frequently a return to (or a revisiting of) fundamental attributes: A juxtaposition of shots that are greater than the sum of its parts educates in the earliest concepts of cinema. And, of course, the ballad construction presents a predictive look to the music video.

THE *EASY RIDER* MOMENT: 0:09:16–0:10:13

The late-starting head credits continue as Wyatt and Billy pull up to a rural motel. A red sign illuminates "Vacancy." Billy rings an unassuming tricycle-like bell centered on his motorcycle's handlebar. A man steps outside to have a look. Wyatt calls above the cycle engines, "Hey, you got a room?" The man turns and goes back inside, letting the office door slam. Wyatt shouts, "Hey, man!" The sign displays larger letters advising "No" over the now blinking "Vacancy." Wyatt gives one last try. "You got a room?" The bikers turn to screen left and, as the last of the opening credits end, Billy raises a gloved finger toward the motel office door. "You asshole!" They ride into the darkness. In a hyper-flickering series of cuts — a sort of six frames on and six off — Wyatt and Billy sit at a campfire, and at once ride off into the black surroundings twice again, before the glittering transition settles on the campfire scene and Billy's rendition of "Going down to Mardi Gras. I'm going to get me a Mardi Gras queen."

The film's editor, Donn Cambern, has explained that neither a straight cut nor a dissolve was fulfilling, and the six-frame-back-and-forth-three-times was "discovered." It is worth noting that the motorcycle engines' track plays across the incoming campfire frames as well as the frames of the outgoing motel scene; and far-off dog barks begin to dominate. It is also worthy to note that Columbia Pictures' chairman of the board, Leo Jaffe, responded after his private screening, "I don't know what the fuck this picture means, but I know we're going to make a fuck of a lot of money!"

*Eyes are vocal, tears have tongues
and there are words not made with lungs.*

— *Richard Crashaw (1613–1649)*

LAST WORD

Richard Crashaw's words predate movies by some 250 years, offering portend aplenty to cinema's bona fides. Director István Szabó has presented a particularly lucid underpinning for film's distinctive benefit: "Words are better in literature; Form, Light, Shadow, Colors are better in painting; Acting is better when [in a] play written by Shakespeare; Emotions are better [expressed] in music. So, if you can't find something unique [in film], something that is original then why do it? Yet audiences love film. Why? I think the speciality of the feature film — that other art cannot show — is that the human face can carry charismatic power and energy."

Szabó's words proffer a more accurate truth when watched and heard on the *Colonel Redl* DVD, under an extra entitled "The Naked Face: Conversations with Director István Szabó and Star Klaus Maria Brandauer": a good case of an idea made more concise via inflection.

Ingmar Bergman tendered a more poetic notion: "I touched wordless secrets that only the cinema can discover."

In this, there is a link to mime acting, and immediately (for me) Marcel Marceau comes to mind — he and Giulietta Masina fixed. A long history precedes the great French mime: British pantomime is a style of humorous entertainment — a Christmastime tradition — presenting a folk or children's tale in jokes, songs, and dancing. And Roman pantomime (ancient Rome) was a theatrical presentation by a single masked actor portraying a story's many characters by way of dance, gesture, and expression, utilizing a chorus to narrate the tale.

Notwithstanding Sergei Eisenstein's apprehension that the invention that permitted "talking pictures" would be used "for highly cultured dramas and other photographed performances of a theatrical sort... [and] will destroy the culture of montage," nor István Szabó's conversation in which he excludes theater, the spoken word, and dance, veracity maintains that screenwriters, directors, actors, cinematographers, and editors have harvested sparkling moments in setting, rhythm, and *words* — ironic and literal — impressed in our collective memory. And let's not forget — it is assuredly what stirred the moment to memory — we *saw* the words *said*.

Speak up!

CASABLANCA (1942)

"The most romantic picture ever made? The best film to come out of a Hollywood studio ever? More an icon than a work of art, [it] is still a thoroughly entertaining romantic melodrama, flawlessly directed, subtly played, lovingly evoking our collective daydreams about lost chances and lost love.... Everything about [the movie] is just right — it seems to have been filmed under a lucky star."
— *movies.tvguide.com*

"Against an electric background of a sleek café in a North African port, through which swirls a backwash of connivers, crooks, and fleeing European refugees, the Warner Brothers are telling a rich, suave, exciting, and moving tale in their new film, which opened at the Hollywood yesterday. They have used Mr. Bogart's personality to inject a cold point of tough resistance to evil forces afoot in Europe today. And they have so combined sentiment, humor, and pathos with taut melodrama and bristling intrigue that the result is a highly entertaining and even inspiring film."
— Bosley Crowther, *New York Times*, November 27, 1942

"The centre of intrigue in old Casablanca, we learn, was Rick's, a night spot where forged passports flowed like water. Into this dive, operated by Bogart, come Henreid, as the leader of an underground movement in Europe, and Miss Bergman, as Europe's most beautiful woman. Henreid has escaped from a concentration camp and is trying to get to America. The Germans would like to stop him by fair means or unwholesome. Claude Rains, as the local police chief, sits cheerfully on the fence and won't do much for anybody. Bogart and Bergman have met before in Paris, it turns out, and they become particularly melancholy whenever the song, 'As Time Goes By' is played.... There is enough topical truth in the picture to suit the topical-minded. Not to speak of the eternal truths always to be found in the better screenplays."
— David Lardner, *New Yorker*, November 28, 1942

"Ingrid Bergman (Mrs. Victor Lazslo) walks into [Rick's] café with her husband, and from their table she spots Sam, the Negro pianist, Rick's only intimate. Sam spots Ingrid too, and his glance is nervous. When Lazslo leaves the room for a moment, he crosses to her quickly. 'Leave him alone!' he begs. 'Leave him alone, Miss Ilse!' And we hold our breath."

— Barbara Deming, "The Reluctant War Hero," *Running Away from Myself: A Dream Portrait of America Drawn from the Films of the 1940s* (1969)

The *TV Guide* database assessment — via questions — awards the movie a prominent place in film and cultural history. The film's dialogue and lyrics have conferred notable durability on the gathering place of memories as certainly as Rick's Café Américain is the "centre of intrigue" in 1941 Casablanca. I have made it a point to include the above reminiscences because together they track the arrangements in story, place, and character and therefore the enduring enchantment of this memorable movie.

The "eternal truths... found in the better screenplays" owe, at the least, a soupçon of gratitude to Murray Burnett and Joan Alison, authors of the play *Everybody Comes to Rick's*. The stirring scene of "the mighty Marseillaise" and the fog-consumed airdrome conclusion notwithstanding, the spoken word and the song of Herman "Dodo" Hupfeld — written for the 1931 Broadway show *Everybody's Welcome* — control the movie as confidently as they would a live staging.

THE *CASABLANCA* MOMENTS

By way of Ilsa's early encounter with Sam — her request "Play it, Sam" (0:32:18) initiates the celebrated "As Time Goes By" — and Rick's later insistence, "You played it for her, now play it for me. Play it!" (0:38:06), the line "Play it again, Sam" was prompted though never actually spoken. Memorable (though inaccurate) phrases signify the quintessence of their moment; their resilience is drawn from spurred imitations. In the case of *Casablanca*, for example, there's Woody Allen's play (1969) and film (1972) *Play it Again, Sam*. But the imitations simply reiterated the predictable phrase of stand-up comics and impersonators throughout television's variety programming of the 1950s, depicting one of their favorites, Humphrey Bogart.

The Hupfeld song had several verses ahead of the *Casablanca* rendering, but starting the song as Sam (Dooley Wilson) instructs, "You

must remember this," made the movie easily affix to (and command) long-term memory.

The movie's screenwriters, Julius J. and Philip G. Epstein and Howard Koch, gushed with gems:

"Of all the gin joints in all the towns in all the world, she walks into mine." (0:37:47)

"Louis, I think this is the beginning of a beautiful friendship." (1:42:02)

The most repeated line in the movie, correctly phrased by comics, writers, movie buffs, and ready lovers, is "Here's looking at you, kid" (0:39:57, 0:43:11, 1:25:22, and 1:37:33), each time said by Bogart to Ingrid Bergman — always with affection, in inflections of tribute, times past, and sacrifice.

The movie offered gallant respite from a war not yet certain in outcome.

Let me mention — with a wish that preserves passion over premise — that in the line about "gin joints," my computer green zig-zagged the last "all the" and recommended "entire." And I thought, of all the computers and all the scriptwriting software in *all the* world, Word comes up with this!

THE TREASURE OF THE SIERRA MADRE
(1948)

"Arguably John Huston's greatest film. Both [the] director and his distinguished [actor] father Walter won Oscars, the only time father and son won the coveted gold statuettes."
—movies.tvguide.com

"Greed, a despicable passion out of which other base ferments may spawn, is seldom treated in the movies with the frank and ironic contempt that is vividly manifested toward it in [this movie], but don't let this note of intelligence distract your attention that [director] Huston is putting it over in a most vivid and exciting action display. Even the least perceptive patron should find this a swell adventure film."
— Bosley Crowther, *New York Times*, January 24, 1948

"We are plumped into the company of a pair of young bums and an ancient prospector scrabbling along in marginal style in the Mexican town of Tampico. The prospector is a great one for getting off windy pronouncements about the effect of gold on the human character, but once he and his chums have gathered together enough cash to finance an expedition, they plunge enthusiastically into the wilds to look for the shiny root of all evil. Up to this point the picture is not too preposterous, but when the boys start shouldering their way through the wilderness, it becomes rather trying."
— John McCarten, *New Yorker*, January 24, 1948

John Huston's film was my earliest movie "treasure," watched with hobbylike ecstasy, over and over, on my family's thirteen-and-a-half-inch Motorola television set, which sat in the kitchen to the left of the refrigerator. Lucky for me, the movie must have also been a favorite of the local New York TV channels, what with the near-daily showings in 1953 and 1954, between the evening hours of four and seven.

While a dozen moments might quickly flick in my head at the sound of the movie's title, in whole or in part, the most memorable, for more than sixty years, is the one that led to unending referenced imitations — though not quite accurate — of actor Alfonso Bedoya.

THE TREASURE OF THE SIERRA MADRE MOMENT: 1:07:06–1:07:31

Bandits arrive at the campsite guarded by Howard, Curtin, and Dobbs — and Cody, an unwelcome visitor who hopes to be let in on their prospecting deeds. One bandit advances. Dobbs shouts "Halto! Halto!" The leader, Gold Hat, is whistled forward by his compadre. Dobbs' eyes show above a boulder, his rifle barrel pointed upward. Gold Hat avows that he and his men are "Federales. You know, the mounted police." Dobbs asks, "If you're the police, where are your badges?" Actor Alfonso Bedoya (Gold Hat) delivers his timeless reply:

"Badges? We ain't got no badges. We don't need no badges. I don't have to show you any stinking badges!"

Though Gold Hat was grammatically correct in his last line — he did *not* use *no* (any) double negative — comics, critics, pundits, and reporters promptly invented a countrywide aside by reducing the four lines to "We don't need no stinking badges!" Eventually "badges" was swapped for any and all things, appropriately dismissed — with cheer — in annoyance or irony: "We don't need no stinking permit!" "I don't need no stinking ticket!" "I don't need no stinking photo ID!" There seems no end of context to a Gold Hat retort.

In February 2009, the Republican Party selected Louisiana governor Bobby Jindal to offer a response to President Barack Obama's address to a joint session of Congress. Jindal was among the few governors — all Republican — to declare that they would reject stimulus money from Washington, D.C. CNN commentator Jack Cafferty reacted, "When you're a state as wealthy as Louisiana, you don't need no stinking stimulus money."

ON THE WATERFRONT (1954)

"The realistic dialogue is poetic in its simplicity.... It is all the more grim and hard-hitting because of the steel-gray look of cinematographer [Boris] Kaufman's startling, neo-documentary approach. A controversial film of its time because of its violence, raw language,... and its daring in representing labor unions in a negative light."
— *movies.tvguide.com*

"While this explosive indictment of the vultures [at] the docksides, unveiled at the Astor yesterday, occasionally is only surface dramatization and an oversimplification of the personalities and evils of our waterfront, it is, nevertheless, an uncommonly powerful, exciting, and imaginative use of the screen by gifted professionals."
— A. H. Weiler, *New York Times*, July 29, 1954

"I'd give cozy odds that no actor this year is going to match Mr. Brando's performance here. [Screenwriter Budd] Schulberg, I've been informed, used to own a piece of a fighter, has garnished [the film] with a good deal of pugilistic argot, and he — or maybe Mr. Kazan — has had the courage to include in the cast such battlers as Tony Galento, Tami Mauriello, and Abe Simon. All of them, it seems to me, do better here than they ever did in the ring. I must say a word about the score by Leonard Bernstein, composed to accompany this movie. It is at once pertinent and unobtrusive, and it always serves to step up the dramatic points the film is making."
— John McCarten, *New Yorker*, July 31, 1954

The prototypical Marlon Brando impersonation likely derives from Tennessee Williams' *A Streetcar Named Desire* — those born after 1965 would probably fix on *The Godfather* for a Brando aural reference — but the beautifully beseeching Terry Malloy's insistence that his brother Charley acknowledge his failing fidelity has provided phrases comical and profound in a timbre similar to that of Stanley Kowalski — somewhere in the high-nasal range and, most especially, spot-on Brando mannerisms.

Gangster union boss Johnny Friendly is under threat of investigation by a crime commission and sends his corrupt lawyer, Charley (Rod Steiger), to convince (with sureness) brother Terry not to give damaging testimony.

The brothers sit in the backseat of a taxi. Charley insists that Terry's promising boxing career was wrecked because a "Skunk for a manager... brought you along too fast."

Terry won't sit for the excuse. "It wasn't him, Charley, it was you! 'Kid, this ain't your night. We're going for the price on Wilson.'"

THE *ON THE WATERFRONT* MOMENT: 1:14:30–1:15:03

Terry is brash about the sources of his life's setbacks. "You was my brother, Charley. You should have looked out for me a little bit. You should have taken care of me so I didn't have to take them dives for the short-end money."

Charley's warped self-righteousness won't allow him to get it. "I had some bets down for you.... You saw some money."

Terry's dedication to truthful testimony is evident. "You don't understand! I could have had class! *I could have been a contender*. I could have been somebody, instead of a bum, which is what I am — let's face it. It was you, Charley."

"I could have been a contender!" or expectedly, "I could *of* been a contender," rings across a half century and more.

A recent HBO sports documentary, *Assault in the Ring* (2009), proves the "Terry in the Taxi" moment's enduring force: Fate, in the hands of the gods, or treacheries (unforeseen) thwart our attainments. Luis Resto, a promising prize fighter ensnared in shameful disgrace via the scheme of his trainer, Panama Lewis, was banned from the sport for tampering with the padding in his boxing gloves. Both fighter and trainer served two years in prison — both insisting on their innocence — following conviction for the vicious beating meted out to Billy Collins Jr., a talented welterweight opponent, on June 16, 1983, at Madison Square Garden. Resto comes clean to the filmmakers, acknowledging that just before the fight, padding was removed from his boxing gloves, and he further confesses to a hand wrap infused with a hardening plaster.

Yet, after owning up to such merciless conduct, Resto abandons accountability, pledging, "Like they say in the movie, I could have been a *champion*."

The line is, of course, "I could have been a *contender*."

Now near destitute, Resto pathetically mimics the movie, but with the shameless immodesty of our new century.

On the Waterfront was adapted from the Pulitzer Prize–winning articles of Malcolm Johnson. The movie delivered actors Rod Steiger and Eva Marie Saint and composer Leonard Bernstein to the silver screen, and during the next decade, Steiger took up residence but a few blocks from the Brooklyn waterfront.

On an afternoon in the autumn of 1966 (or so), I was on my way into Manhattan from my family's Garden Place apartment in Brooklyn Heights when, reaching the corner at Joralemon Street, I caught sight of Rod Steiger and his wife, Claire Bloom, descending the stoop steps of their building. She was dressed with such decisive sophistication that two things at once looked inconsistent: no limousine waiting curbside and Steiger's incongruous presence.

Claire Bloom wore a satiny-combed black fur coat and pearls and earrings that, adding to her beyond-belief complexion, indicated a celebration of a Broadway opening, or a gathering of nominees selected for stage or film awards. Rod Steiger, on the other hand, was wearing a full-length woolen outer coat, similar in style to his costuming in the taxi cab scene. Unrelated to the frayed look of the thing, he was not wearing trousers. His legs were bare, with feet in slippers, and he was in need of a shave, but not the sort of "need" made fashionable by advertising men or screenwriters. No, his cheeks and chin were stubbly clear of style, and his hair was so mussed — or static packed — that tufts pointed east and west and north.

All together, Steiger had let loose his standing and "instead" looked like "a bum," which *wasn't* what he was.

How could this husband attend to his wife and the appointed glamour in such poor shape?

They turned left on Joralemon, and, my nosiness enticing, I followed. We all walked to Montague Street (the business thoroughfare in the Heights), and they entered a deli. I stood alongside them at the counter, pretending I was trying to decide on a purchase.

Rod Steiger and Claire Bloom ordered sandwich meat varieties in weights of a quarter and half pounds. When they exited, I followed; they went straight home.

Why, I wondered, would any woman prepare with such elegance to pick up cold cuts? I turned around and walked to the subway station at the Saint George Hotel.

SOME LIKE IT HOT (1959)

"Nobody's perfect — except Billy Wilder in top form. One of the most well loved of Hollywood comedies, Wilder's masterly spoof of gangster films and gender roles revels in invention and effervescent high camp."
—*movies.tvguide.com*

"There should be no doubt this morning that the members of the happily irreverent film troupe that made [this film] have done something constructive about the old wheeze that begins, "Who was that lady I saw you with?" For, in fashioning this overlong, occasionally labored, but often outrageously funny series of variations on an ancient gag, they have come up with a rare, rib-tickling lampoon that should keep them, the customers, and the management of the newly refurbished Loews State, which reopened yesterday, chortling with glee."
— A. H. Weiler, *New York Times*, March 30, 1959

"A jolly carefree enterprise, in which some of the old phrenetic nonsense of Max Sennet is restored to the screen. The result of a scriptural collabora-tion between Billy Wilder and I. A. L. Diamond, the picture brings back the madcap days of the twenties.... A pair of seedy musicians — a saxophon-ist and a bass player, who have [witnessed] a variation on the St. Valentine's Day massacre in Chicago — are for safety's sake compelled to head South disguised as members of an all-girl band.... The antics of [the] two, once they are flung in with the harem that a sultan might envy, are funny and altogether unobjectionable. En route by train from Chicago to Miami, the lads are sorely tempted by both wine and women (the all-girl band includes quite a few lushes), but they behave, however reluctantly, with a restraint that would win the admiration of St. Anthony."
— John McCarten, *New Yorker*, April 4, 1959

"Josephine" (Tony Curtis) and "Daphne" (Jack Lemmon) scarcely beat the gangsters out of the Miami hotel, winding up with Sugar Kane (Marilyn Monroe) and Osgood E. Fielding III (Joe E. Brown) in a motorboat heading from the dock to billionaire Fielding's anchored yacht and a planned wedding to Daphne. Monroe and Curtis, seated at the stern, cuddle in a long kiss. Sugar has only just learned that he is neither Josephine nor a wealthy suitor — just unadorned Joe, a saxophonist — but Sugar adores him even so. At the helm, Osgood, still certain that Daphne is a genuine bass-playing *woman*, blissfully announces: "I called Mama. She was so happy she cried. She wants you to have her wedding gown. It's white lace!" Daphne (really Jerry) replies in stammer-starts and an anxious giggle, "I can't get married in your mother's dress.... She and I.... We are not built the same way." In as large a grin as anyone ever grinned, Osgood answers instantly, and sensibly, "We can have it altered." Daphne declares steadfastly, "Osgood, I'm gonna level with you. We can't get married at all." After Osgood asks, "Why not?" there begins a long list of Daphne objections and Osgood remedies.

THE *SOME LIKE IT HOT* MOMENT: 2:00:17–2:00:53

Daphne: "Well? In the first place, I'm not a natural blonde."

Osgood: "Doesn't matter."

Daphne: "I smoke. I smoke all the time!"

Osgood: "I don't care."

Daphne: "I've a terrible past; for three years now, I've been living with a saxophone player."

Osgood: "I forgive you."

Daphne: "I can never have children."

Osgood: "We can adopt some."

Daphne: "Well.... You don't understand, Osgood! Ahhh!" Lemmon removes his wig, thumps Osgood on the chest, ceases the falsetto voice, and grumbles, "I'm a man!"

Osgood: "Well.... No one's perfect!"

The startled Jerry can't quite burble a response. Osgood beams and affectionately turns to Jerry, as the white comical font displaying "The End" and the chipper sweet tune wrap the movie.

Some Like It Hot, nominated for six Academy Awards, is ranked the number one comedy of all time by the American Film Institute and was chosen by AFI as one of the 100 Best Films in history. Director Billy Wilder has said, "You have to be orderly to shoot disorder; this was the best disorder we ever had."

A half century ago — a measurement in time that feels a lot longer than fifty years —Wilder's (and I. A. L. Diamond's) screenplay, comprising protagonist "cross-dressers" — an expression less contentious (or hot) than "transvestite" — and bawdy sexual "restraint" was estimated to be an "altogether unobjectionable" "rib-tickling lampoon" of "chortling glee." The last words of the movie have been recognized by the American Film Institute.

On a late night in 1959, with little exploratory prospect, several friends and I attended night court in lower Manhattan. The episodes, presented (before a judge) in the public domain, might be the inspiration for Jerry Springer and other reality programming of late twentieth-century television. In particular, one "perp" locked Wilder's and Diamond's last words: A gruff though stylishly dressed man, busted for operating a gambling ring, sought forgiving dismissal or, at the least, the court's lenience by emphasizing, "This is the very first time I've been in trouble with the law." The judge was well prepared and, reading from a fat folder, recited date and incident of a half-dozen previous misdemeanors and half as many felony convictions. "Well, Mr. Gruff," the judge asked, "for someone who claims never to have 'been in trouble with the law,' what do you have to say for yourself?"

"Your honor... whom among us is perfect?"

Some Like It Hot just celebrated its golden anniversary.

Oh, how I hate my mind,
all those memories
that have invented their own memories.
— Alan Michael Parker

FINALE:
MOMENTS,
MEMORY,
MEMORABLE

I n the year my uncle introduced me to the movies, the Loews movie house that projected the disturbing death of Barbara Stanwyck's Leona was itself beamed onto screens when the Williamsburg Bridge's generous Delancey Street access was captured in a vérité detective movie directed by Jules Dassin.

THE NAKED CITY (1948)

"This superlative film set the patterns for myriad documentary-type dramas to come. Its producer, [Mark] Hellinger, patterned the tale after the tabloid newspaper stories he wrote in his youth, and he narrates the picture with the same kind of terse but poignant vitality that was the hallmark of his sensational prose. Shot completely on location in New York City, [the film] chronicles the grim urban landscape and depicts its everyday life and citizens."

— *movies.tvguide.com*

"A good many realistic views of Manhattan pinned down by a competent camera, distinguish [this] film produced by the late Mark Hellinger, whose [narration] is about as penetrating as the spiel of a guide on a sightseeing bus, and the film resorts to all kinds of flummery to force the real complexities of New York to the simple and sentimental concept of the city so often set forth in the Broadway columns."

— John McCarten, *New Yorker*, March 13, 1948

"The post-War realistic period [of film noir] tended toward the problems of crime in the streets, political corruption and police routine. The realistic urban look of this phase is seen in such films as *The Killers, Union Station, Force of Evil, Dead Reckoning, Cry of the City, The Set-Up, Brute Force, Ruthless,* and *The Naked City.*"

— Paul Schrader, "Notes on Film Noir," *Film Comment* 8, no. 1
    (Spring 1972)

It would compel some detective work to clarify how the database summary could credit producer Mark Hellinger's narration with a "terse but poignant vitality" when McCarten's review blames the narration for meaningless sentiments "often set forth in the Broadway columns." The *New Yorker* critic's assessment is fitting in that Hellinger not only wrote such tabloid stuff himself but was inspired by tabloid crime photographer Arthur Fellig's (aka Weegee) book of "corpses and fires and arrests and crowds and spectacles" entitled *Naked City*. The difference between praise and complaint is the product of individual receptiveness, often contained within cultural (artistic) eras. It is most intriguing, in this case, because McCarten's sensibilities are likely ahead of their time.

At the start of the film's climactic chase sequence, bad guy Willie Garzah is running scared at the Manhattan entrance to the Williamsburg Bridge when uniformed and plainclothes cops fill the street. Garzah checks the surroundings, looking to flee, and this initiates a POV pan.

The camera's sweep shows the Loews Apollo just past the imposing facade of the NYPD's Third Precinct.

Garzah makes his escape, running up and onto the pedestrian walkway of the bridge, and collides with a blind man and his dog; the master shot shows the Loews Delancey in the upper right distance of the frame.

On that production day, the mother of my first friend, David Cohen, was on the Williamsburg Bridge's pedestrian walkway, strolling with her new baby in her carriage, when a wild bunch ran past: It was Willie Garzah and the Jules Dassin film crew.

When the film hit the screen, all the adults from the neighborhood lined up. I can recall great neighborhood squabbles, some swearing that they did see Mrs. Cohen on the big screen, others swearing at them, insisting, "She wasn't there!"

In the month of my twenty-second birthday, I began entry to a film career. Hired by a postproduction company in the Film Center Building and knowing absolutely nothing, I asked for reading recommendations to go hand in hand with the training kindly provided me by experienced employees. I purchased, as advised, Karel Reisz's book *The Technique of Film Editing*. The first edition was released in the early 1950s and was among the very few books to pay full attention to the art and craft of the editor. Reisz, a former editor turned director, makes good use of moments in movies to illustrate specific concepts. One of his selections is from *The Naked City*.

I thumbed my way through, and in a flash, as in the days of old-time motion flipcards, I caught site of Mrs. Cohen. In 1968 Karel Reisz was joined by Gavin Millar to produce a second edition. Mrs. Cohen hadn't changed a bit! After five decades you can find her in the ninth still (identified as #20), on page 73.

THE NAKED CITY MOMENT: 1:30:16

David's mom and sister enter and vanish in just two frames!

Luc Sante, writing the notes for the Criterion Collection DVD of *The Naked City*, describes the crafty production work and verifies (for me) the movie's immediate and historical influences: "Some scenes [were shot] with a camera concealed in a van, others apparently through two-way mirrors. [It] is the teeming, unscripted life of the city that gives the movie its sweep and its intrinsic documentary interest. You see kids jumping into the river from the docks and playing games on the walkway of the Williamsburg Bridge, horses pulling milk wagons and peddler's carts, El trains rattling overhead in lower Manhattan, pretzel vendors displaying their wares on sticks, laborers going about their trades. Such things are now vanished and thus exotic. At the time, they were common sights, but even for city dwellers who passed them everyday, their presence in a movie confirmed their reality in a new and unexpected way."

With an eye alert to relevant bits and pieces while writing this book, I came across a full-page ad in the *New York Times*, persuading us to "Revisit New York's Good Old Days…. Celebrate a bygone era of New York, when movies were a nickel and horse-drawn wagons roamed the streets. These historical images from The New York Times Store are available as exhibition quality photographs." I had seen similar advertisements offering a selection of beautiful black-and-white shots, but this ad caught my attention. On the *Times'* page was *The Five-Cent Movie House, 1917*, picture from the New York Times Photo Archive (NSAPM12). The Comet Theatre was located on Third Avenue, and a banner across the marquee reads, "High Class Motion Pictures & Illustrated Songs." Large posters crowd the entranceway, and the *Times* reports that the theater claimed "practically a two-hour show." Nineteen hundred and seventeen? The good old days? Just slightly more than thirty years later, I got to see a full eight-hour show for a dime.

I make no claim here of *my* "good old days," though I must admit to many fond memories of the post-WWII Lower East Side. I can't recall that "the problems of crime in the streets" ruffled me or my family; nor did the cinematic notion of film noir mean a thing to me for another dozen years.

"Moments," "memory," and "memorable" are, above all, measurements. *Moments* can be a consequence of the precise: a second or a minute; a jiffy, a split second, or a flash; a "feel" in duration or perception.

Memory can be reckoned in capacity for recall, or in remembrances or reminiscences, but memory is neither static nor absolute; it can be transformed when summoned to mind, or in a re-summoning. And, though *memorable* might be defined as "worth remembering" beyond our efforts to memorize, seldom do moments imprint in the mind as conscious choice. Unforgettable, outstanding, or impressive are measured addendums postwitness: a human archiving instinct. Memory is history.

The writing (and research) of this movie memoir yielded recollections that, without purposeful assist from me, gave way to a bounty of seasoned, yet fresh, surprises. Accessible connections bring me to this:

Set aside Blatty and Freidkin's assertion on why people go to the movies. The heritable allure of story shimmers in the closing lines of poet Ann Pierson Wiese's "Tell Me."

Riding a subway train, early in the morning, Wiese takes notice of a homeless man waking after a night's sleep on the train. The man tidily folds his blanket, begins grooming, and substitutes his soiled clothing for garments less grubby:

Whoever you are — tell me what unforgiving series
of moments has added up to this one: a man
making himself presentable to the world in front
of the world, as if life has revealed to him the secret
that all our secrets from one another are imaginary.

The span of life is waning fast;
Beware, unthinking youth, beware!
Thy soul's eternity depends
Upon the record moments bear!

— Eliza Cook

BIBLIOGRAPHY

Berger, Joseph. Obituary. "Albert Shanker, 68, Combative Leader who Transformed Teachers' Union Dies." *New York Times*, Monday, February 24, 1997.

Bergman, Ingmar. *Images: My Life in Film*. Translated by Marianne Ruuth. New York: Arcade Publishing, 1994.

Burrough, Bryan. "Outlaws in Love." *New York Times Book Review*, May 10, 2009.

Cook, John. *The Book of Positive Quotations*. New York: Gramercy Books, 1993

Edelman, Rob. *Alexander Nevsky: Eisenstein's Symphonic Vision*. Riegelsville, PA: Corinth Films, 1988.

Fox, Ken, and Maitland McDonagh, eds. *Film & Video Companion*. New York: Barnes and Noble Books, 2004.

Giddins, Gary. "Still Curious." Criterion Collection, March 10, 2003, *www.criterion.com*.

Greenspun, Roger. Screen. "*Where's Poppa?* Aims to Remove Bachelor's Momma." Review of *Where's Poppa?* (1970), *New York Times Review*, November 11, 1970, *www.movies.nytimes.com/movie/review*.

Groopman, Jerome. *How Doctors Think*. Boston: Houghton Mifflin, 2007.

Guare, John. Collaborations. "John Guare on Louis Malle." *New Yorker*, March 21, 1994.

HBO. Sports of the 20th Century. *Assault in the Ring*. New York: Live Star Entertainment, 2009.

Holden, Stephen. "A Mule's Long Trek in Search of the North American Dream." Review of *Maria Full of Grace* (2003), *New York Times Review*, July 16, 2004.

Kehr, Dave. DVDs. *Indelible '60s Memories*. Arts & Leisure, *New York Times*, June 21, 2009.

Lane, Anthony. The Film File. Review of *Caché* (Hidden). *New Yorker*, January 9, 2006, *www.newyorker.com/arts/reviews/film*.

Lopate, Phillip, ed. *American Movie Critics: An Anthology From the Silents Until Now*. New York: Library of America, 2006.

Mackendrick, Alexander. *On Film-Making: An Introduction to the Craft of the Director*. New York: Faber and Faber, 2004.

Macmillan Dictionary of Quotations. New York: Macmillan Publishing Company, 1987.

Menand, Louis. A Critic at Large. "It Took a Village: How the Voice Changed Journalism." *New Yorker*, January 5, 2009.

Mitchell, Richard. "King Kong." *Films in Review* (January 1975).

Murch, Walter. *In the Blink of an Eye: A Perspective on Film Editing*. 2nd ed. Los Angeles: Silman-James Press, 1995.

New York Times. The Arts. "Revisit New York's Good Old Days," advertisement, April 25, 2009, *www.nytstore.com*.

Nichols, Peter M., ed. *The New York Times Guide to the Best 1,000 Movies Ever Made*. New York: St. Martin's Griffin, 2004.

Pepperman, Richard D. *Film School: How to Watch DVDs and Learn Everything About Filmmaking*. Studio City, CA: Michael Wiese Productions, 2008.

Pollizzotti, Mark. "*Last Year at Marienbad*: Which Year at Where?" Criterion Collection, June 23, 2009, *www.criterion.com*.

Rebello, Stephen, and Richard Allen. *Reel Art: Great Posters from the Golden Age of the Silver Screen*. New York and London: Abbeville Press, 1988.

Reisz, Karel, and Gavin Millar. *The Technique of Film Editing*. 2nd ed. London: Focal Press, 1968.

Remnick, David. Introduction. *The Complete New Yorker*. New York: Random House, 2005.

Rowin, Michael Joshua. *La Strada*. Essential Art House [credits]. New York: Criterion Collection, 2008.

Sacks, Oliver. *Musicophilia: Tales of Music and the Brain*. New York: Alfred A. Knopf, 2007.

Sante, Luc. "*The Naked City:* New York Plays Itself." Criterion Collection, March 19, 2007, *www.criterion.com*.

Schrader, Paul. "Notes on Film Noir." *Film Comment* 8, no. 1 (Spring 1972).

Scott, A. O. "A Nice Middle-Class Couple With Their Own Stalker." Review of *Caché* (Hidden) (2005), *New York Times Review*, December 23, 2005, *www.movies.nytimes.com*.

Scott, A. O. "Sorrowful Knowledge and Startled Innocence in Franco's Spain." Review of *The Spirit of the Beehive* (1973), *New York Times Review*, January 27, 2006, *www.movies.nytimes.com*.

Smith, Paul Julian. "*The Spirit of the Beehive:* Spanish Lessons." Criterion Collection, September 18, 2006, *www.criterion.com*.

Starz Encore Entertainment, TCEP, and the American Cinema Editors (ACE). *The Cutting Edge: The Magic of Movie Editing*. Warner Home Video, 2005.

Sullivan, Monica. *VideoHound's Independent Film Guide*. 2nd ed. Detroit: Visible Ink Press, 1999.

Turrent, Tomás Pérez, and José de la Colina. "The Return to Spain." Excerpted from *Objects of Desire: Conversations with Luis Buñuel*. New York: Criterion Collection, 2006.

Vaz, Mark Cotta. *Living Dangerously: The Adventures of Merrian C. Cooper*. New York: Random House, 2005.

Wood, Michael. "*Viridiana*: The Human Comedy." Criterion Collection, May 22, 2006, *www.criterion.com*.

FILMOGRAPHY I (A–Z)

12 Angry Men: 1957 • United Artists • B&W • 95 min.

400 Blows, The: 1959 • Janus Films • B&W • 93 min.

2001: A Space Odyssey: 1968 • Metro-Goldwyn-Mayer • Color • 160 min.

Alexander Nevsky: 1938 • Mosfilm • B&W • 107 min.

Amadeus: 1984 • Orion • Color • 158 min.

Apocalypse Now: 1979 • United Artists • Color • 153 min.

Atlantic City: 1980 • Paramount • Color • 104 min.

Blow-Up: 1966 • Premier Pictures • Color • 110 min.

Bonnie and Clyde: 1967 • Warner Brothers • Color • 111 min.

Breathless: 1960 • Films Around the World • B&W • 89 min.

Bridge on the River Kwai, The: 1957 • Columbia • Color • 161 min.

Butch Cassidy and the Sundance Kid: 1969 • Twentieth Century-Fox • Color • 112 min.

Caché: 2005 • Sony Pictures Classics• Color • 121 min.

Casablanca: 1942 • Warner Brothers • B&W • 102 min.

Chinatown: 1974 • Paramount • Color • 131 min.

Cinema Paradiso: 1988 • Cristaldifilm • Color • 123 min.

Colonel Redl: 1985 • Mafilm Objektiv • Color • 144 min.

Dog Day Afternoon: 1975 • Artists Entertainment • Color • 130 min.

Easy Rider: 1969 • Columbia • Color • 94 min.

Exorcist, The: 1973 • Warner Brothers • Color • 121 min.

Fanny and Alexander: 1983 • Embassy Pictures • Color • 188 min.

French Connection, The: 1971 • Twentieth Century-Fox • Color • 104 min.

Gold Rush, The: 1925 • Charles Chaplin-UA Production • B&W • 96 min.

High Noon: 1952 • United Artists • B&W • 85 min.

Hiroshima Mon Amour: 1959 • Zenith International • B&W • 88 min.

I Am Curious — Yellow: 1967 • Criterion • B&W • 121 min.

Ikiru: 1952 • Brandon Films • B&W • 141 min.

Ju Dou: 1990 • Miramax • Color • 94 min.

King Kong: 1933 • RKO Pictures • B&W • 100 min.

La Strada: 1954 • Trans-Lux Films • B&W • 115 min.

Last of the Mohicans, The: 1936 • Small • B&W • 91 min.

Last Year at Marienbad: 1961 • Terra/Silver-Cineriz • B&W • 94 min.

Lawrence of Arabia: 1962 • Columbia • Color • 220 min.

Marathon Man: 1976 • Paramount • Color • 125 min.

Maria Full of Grace: 2004 • Fine Line Features • Color • 101 min.

Midnight Cowboy: 1969 • United Artists • Color • 119 min.

Naked City, The: 1948 • Universal • B&W • 96 min.

On the Waterfront: 1954 • Columbia • B&W • 108 min.

Paths of Glory: 1957 • United Artists • B&W • 86 min.

Psycho: 1960 • Paramount • B&W • 109 min.

Ran: 1985 • Orion • Color • 160 min.

Sleeper: 1973 • United Artists • Color • 88 min.

Some Like It Hot: 1959 • United Artists • B&W •120 min.

Sorry, Wrong Number: 1948 • Paramount • B&W • 89 min.

Spirit of the Beehive, The: 1973 • Janus Films • Color • 98 min.

Talk to Her: 2002 • Sony Pictures Classics • Color • 113 min.

Treasure of the Sierra Madre, The: 1948 • Warner Brothers • B&W • 126 min.

Under the Sand: 2000 • Arte France Cinema • Color • 95 min.

Viridiana: 1961 • Kingsley Films • B&W • 90 min.

Walk in the Sun, A: 1945 • Twentieth Century-Fox • B&W • 117 min.

Where's Poppa?: 1970 • United Artists • Color • 83 min.

Y tu mamá también: 2001 • IFC Films • Color • 105 min.

Z: 1969 • Cinema V • Color • 127 min.

FILMOGRAPHY II
(1925–2005)

1925: *The Gold Rush* • Charles Chaplin-UA Production • B&W • 96 min.

1933: *King Kong* • RKO Pictures • B&W • 100 min.

1936: *The Last of the Mohicans* • Small • B&W • 91 min.

1938: *Alexander Nevsky* • Mosfilm • B&W • 107 min.

1942: *Casablanca* • Warner Brothers • B&W • 102 min.

1945: *A Walk in the Sun* • Twentieth Century-Fox • B&W • 117 min.

1948: *The Naked City* • Universal • B&W • 96 min.

1948: *Sorry, Wrong Number* • Paramount • B&W • 89 min.

1948: *The Treasure of the Sierra Madre* • Warner Brothers • B&W • 126 min.

1952: *High Noon* • United Artists • B&W • 85 min.

1952: *Ikiru* • Brandon Films • B&W • 141 min.

1954: *La Strada* • Trans-Lux Films • B&W • 115 min.

1954: *On the Waterfront* • Columbia • B&W • 108 min.

1957: *12 Angry Men* • United Artists • B&W • 95 min.

1957: *The Bridge on the River Kwai* • Columbia • Color • 161 min.

1957: *Paths of Glory* • United Artists • B&W • 86 min.

1959: *The 400 Blows* • Janus Films • B&W • 93 min.

1959: Hiroshima Mon Amour • Zenith International • B&W • 88 min.

1959: *Some Like It Hot* • United Artists • B&W •120 min.

1960: *Breathless* • Films Around the World • B&W • 89 min.

1960: *Psycho* • Paramount • B&W • 109 min.

1961: *Last Year at Marienbad* • Terra/Silver-Cineriz • B&W • 94 min.

1961: *Viridiana* • Kingsley Films • B&W • 90 min.

1962: *Lawrence of Arabia* • Columbia • Color • 220 min.

1966: *Blow-Up* • Premier Pictures • Color • 110 min.

1967: *Bonnie and Clyde* • Warner Brothers • Color • 111 min.

1967: *I Am Curious — Yellow* • Criterion • B&W • 121 min.

1968: *2001: A Space Odyssey* • Metro-Goldwyn-Mayer • Color • 160 min.

1969: *Butch Cassidy and the Sundance Kid* • Twentieth Century-Fox • Color • 112 min.

1969: *Easy Rider* • Columbia • Color • 94 min.

1969: *Midnight Cowboy* • United Artists • Color • 119 min.

1969: *Z* • Cinema V • Color • 127 min.

1970: *Where's Poppa?* • United Artists • Color • 83 min.

1971: *The French Connection* • Twentieth Century-Fox • Color • 104 min.

1973: *The Exorcist* • Warner Brothers • Color • 121 min.

1973: *Sleeper* • United Artists • Color • 88 min.

1973: *The Spirit of the Beehive* • Janus Films • Color • 98 min.

1974: *Chinatown* • Paramount • Color • 131 min.

1975: *Dog Day Afternoon* • Artists Entertainment • Color • 130 min.

1976: *Marathon Man* • Paramount • Color • 125 min.

1979: *Apocalypse Now* • United Artists • Color • 153 min.

1980: *Atlantic City* • Paramount • Color • 104 min.

1983: *Fanny and Alexander* • Embassy Pictures • Color • 188 min.

1984: *Amadeus* • Orion • Color • 158 min.

1985: *Colonel Redl* • Mafilm Objektiv • Color • 144 min.

1985: *Ran* • Orion • Color • 160 min.

1988: *Cinema Paradiso* • Cristaldifilm • Color • 123 min.

1990: *Ju Dou* • Miramax • Color • 94 min.

2000: *Under the Sand* • Arte France Cinema • Color • 95 min.

2001: *Y tu mamá también* • IFC Films • Color • 105 min.

2002: *Talk to Her* • Sony Pictures Classics • Color • 113 min.

2004: *Maria Full of Grace* • Fine Line Features • Color • 101 min.

2005: *Caché* • Sony Pictures Classics• Color • 121 min.

INDEX

ABOUT THE AUTHOR

Richard D. Pepperman has worked in film for more than forty-five years. His credits include work as an editor, postproduction supervisor, and consultant on features, documentaries, industrials, and commercials.

Richard's film collaborations have been official selections to many international festivals, including Aspen, Berlin, Cannes, the Hamptons, Karlovy Vary (Czech Republic), London, Montreal, Munich, Rotterdam, Sitges (Barcelona), Tel Aviv, and Toronto.

His collaborations have been honored with an Outstanding Documentary Award by the Academy of Motion Picture Arts & Sciences, an Andy Award, and a Clio Award. Other honors include screenwriting judge for the Nicholl Fellowships, Academy of Motion Picture Arts & Sciences, and Distinguished Artist-Teacher Award from the School of Visual Arts, New York City.

Richard has taught workshops and seminars at Film/Video Arts, the Pratt Institute, and the New School University. He currently teaches the "Art of Editing" at the School of Visual Arts, where he is beginning his thirty-ninth year.

His articles have appeared in *Student Filmmakers Magazine* and on *www.fylmz.com* and *www.writersstore.com*.

Richard is the author of *The Eye is Quicker. Film Editing: Making a Good Film Better* (2004); *Setting Up Your Scenes: The Inner Workings of Great Films* (2005) and *Film School: How to Watch DVDs and Learn Everything About Filmmaking* (2008).

He lives with his wife Betsy, big dog Ollie and small parrot Holly in Monmouth County, New Jersey and Mount Holly, Vermont.

SETTING UP YOUR SCENES
THE INNER WORKINGS
OF GREAT FILMS

RICHARD D. PEPPERMAN

Every great filmmaker has films which inspired him or her to greater and greater heights. Here, for the first time, is an awe-inspiring guide that takes you into the inner workings of classic scenes, revealing the aspects that make them great and the reasons they have served as inspirations.

An invaluable resource for screenwriter, cinematographer, actor, director, and editor, Pepperman's book uses examples from six decades of international films to illustrate what happens when story, character, dialogue, text, subtext, and set-ups come together to create cinematic magic.

With over 400 photos of selected movie clips laid out beautifully in a widescreen format, this book shows you how to emulate the masters and achieve your dreams.

"Setting Up Your Scenes *is both visually stunning and very useful for students of cinema. Its design, layout, and content make the book unique and irresistible.*"
    – Amresh Sinha, New York University/The School of Visual Arts

"*Pepperman has written a book which should form the basis for an intelligent discussion about the basic building blocks of great scenes across a wide variety of films. Armed with the information in this book, teachers, students, filmmakers, and film lovers can begin to understand how good editing and scene construction can bring out the best storytelling to create a better film.*"
    – Norman Hollyn, Associate Professor and Editing Track Head,
      School of Cinema-Television at the University of Southern California

"*Pepperman dissects some very infamous scenes from some very famous movies — providing us with the most breathtaking black and white stills — in order to highlight the importance of the interplay between dialogue, subtext, and shot selection in great filmmaking.*"
    – Lily Sadri, Writer, Screenwriter, *Fixing Fairchild*,
      Contributor to *www.absolutewrite.com*

RICHARD D. PEPPERMAN has been a film editor for more than 40 years and a teacher for more than 30. He is the author of *The Eye Is Quicker* and *Film School*.

$24.95 · 245 PAGES · ORDER NUMBER 42RLS · ISBN: 9781932907087

THE EYE IS QUICKER
FILM EDITING: MAKING A GOOD FILM BETTER

RICHARD D. PEPPERMAN

Did you ever want to know how to apply simple and practical work techniques to all that film editing theory? Here is an authentic "how-to" guide — adaptable to all tools and technologies — to make you a better editor of film or video. This is the most comprehensive book on the principles, methods, and strategies vital to the creative art of film editing.

Pepperman's vibrant approach uses dozens of terrific sequences from a wide array of films to teach you how editing can make a good film better. He defines what is constant in all great work and gives you all the tips you need to achieve your own greatness.

The Eye is Quicker is indispensable for screenwriters, directors, and, of course, film and video editors.

"The qualities that have made Richard so inspiring and beloved a teacher — passion, curiosity, humor, and humility — make this book as alive and enticing as a class or conversation with him. The Eye Is Quicker will benefit future generations of film editors. It is a very good read for film lovers, and a rich mine for practitioners in the other arts."
          — Jennifer Dunning, *New York Times*

"Pepperman brings decades of experience as an editor and teacher to lessons supported by example and illustration. Here is a voice that is caring and supportive. To read The Eye Is Quicker *is to attend a master class."*
          — Vincent LoBrutto, Author, *Stanley Kubrick: A Biography*

"Pepperman not only shares his knowledge of editing's art and craft, he gives wholly of himself — insights, philosophies, humor, and risks of being fully alive to seeing and feeling. To study with Richard is a privilege; to read this book is to receive a profound gift."
          — Louis Phillips, Playwright, Author, *The Last of the Marx Brothers' Writers*

"A highly informative book — stimulating material."
          — Chris Newman, Three-time Academy Award®-Winning
             Production Sound Mixer

RICHARD D. PEPPERMAN is a teacher and thesis advisor at The School Of Visual Arts in New York City. He is the author of *Setting Up Your Scenes* and *Film School*.

$27.95 · 268 PAGES · ORDER NUMBER 116RLS · ISBN: 9780941188845

FILM SCHOOL
HOW TO WATCH DVDS
AND LEARN EVERYTHING ABOUT FILMMAKING

RICHARD D. PEPPERMAN

The smartest professors at the top film schools use DVDs to teach all aspects of filmmaking. But you don't have to plunk down $40,000 to sit in their classroom when you have Richard Pepperman's new book. This amazing resource cuts to the chase with more than six decades of films to watch to learn the most vital concepts in filmmaking. The book is organized by STORY, PLACE, and CHARACTER – utilizing more than 20 topics in the education of actors, cinematographers, directors, editors, production designers, and screenwriters.

Here, in a single volume, is a rich and lively approach for teachers, students, and professionals that builds a strong foundation in understanding the art with its extensive insights into teaching and learning all of filmmaking's disciplines. Fire up your DVD player, you are about to become a Filmmaker by watching scenes from 50 great DVDs.

"Film School *is a result of life experiences, teaching, and a true passion for cinema. It is not an academic dissertation or a technical treatise. Rather, through Richard Pepperman's gifted teaching style, he presents the art of filmmaking as journey. Pepperman shows that a film is the possibility of a true encounter, offering insights equally valuable to the movie buff, aspiring filmmaker, and professional in the field. Finally, filmmaking can be considered 'par coer'!"*
— Simonetta d'Italia-Wiener, Professor of Italian, Crossroads, New York Cultural Center

"*Richard Pepperman's latest book on movies, and moviemaking, provides an abundance of insights.* Film School *is a great book for anyone interested in movies, most especially for those who can't study in a traditional film school program. Here is a wonderful reminder of the great films to be watched, and slowly re-watched, for all the grand little things.* Film School *is a great resource for students of cinema, and all those who love movies!"*
— Robert Hyams, Post-Production Supervisor, LaserPacific Media Corporation

RICHARD D. PEPPERMAN is the author of *The Eye Is Quicker, Film Editing: Making A Good Film Better* and *Setting Up Your Scenes: The Inner Workings Of Great Films*. He has taught at The New School University, Pratt Institute, and Film/Video Arts. He currently teaches at the School of Visual Arts where he is an honored recipient of the Distinguished Artist-Teacher Award.

$24.95 · 264 PAGES · ORDER NUMBER 81RLS · ISBN: 9781932907414

FILM DIRECTING: SHOT BY SHOT
VISUALIZING FROM CONCEPT TO SCREEN

STEVEN D. KATZ

BEST SELLER
OVER 200,000 COPIES SOLD!

Film Directing: Shot by Shot — with its famous blue cover — is the best-known book on directing and a favorite of professional directors as an on-set quick reference guide.

This international bestseller is a complete catalog of visual techniques and their stylistic implications, enabling working filmmakers to expand their knowledge.

Contains in-depth information on shot composition, staging sequences, visualization tools, framing and composition techniques, camera movement, blocking tracking shots, script analysis, and much more.

Includes over 750 storyboards and illustrations, with never-before-published storyboards from Steven Spielberg's *Empire of the Sun*, Orson Welles' *Citizen Kane*, and Alfred Hitchcock's *The Birds*.

"(To become a director) you have to teach yourself what makes movies good and what makes them bad. John Singleton has been my mentor... he's the one who told me what movies to watch and to read Shot by Shot."
— Ice Cube, *New York Times*

"A generous number of photos and superb illustrations accompany each concept, many of the graphics being from Katz' own pen... Film Directing: Shot by Shot *is a feast for the eyes."*
— *Videomaker* Magazine

"... demonstrates the visual techniques of filmmaking by defining the process whereby the director converts storyboards into photographed scenes."
— *Back Stage Shoot*

"Contains an encyclopedic wealth of information."
— *Millimeter* Magazine

STEVEN D. KATZ is an award-winning filmmaker and also the author of *Film Directing: Cinematic Motion*.

$27.95 · 366 PAGES · ORDER NUMBER 7RLS · ISBN: 9780941188104

THE WRITER'S JOURNEY
3RD EDITION

MYTHIC STRUCTURE FOR WRITERS

CHRISTOPHER VOGLER

BEST SELLER
OVER 170,000 COPIES SOLD!

See why this book has become an international best seller and a true classic. *The Writer's Journey* explores the powerful relationship between mythology and storytelling in a clear, concise style that's made it required reading for movie executives, screenwriters, playwrights, scholars, and fans of pop culture all over the world.

Both fiction and nonfiction writers will discover a set of useful myth-inspired storytelling paradigms (i.e., "The Hero's Journey") and step-by-step guidelines to plot and character development. Based on the work of Joseph Campbell, *The Writer's Journey* is a must for all writers interested in further developing their craft.

The updated and revised third edition provides new insights and observations from Vogler's ongoing work on mythology's influence on stories, movies, and man himself.

"This book is like having the smartest person in the story meeting come home with you and whisper what to do in your ear as you write a screenplay. Insight for insight, step for step, Chris Vogler takes us through the process of connecting theme to story and making a script come alive."
> – Lynda Obst, Producer, *Sleepless in Seattle, How to Lose a Guy in 10 Days;*
> Author, *Hello, He Lied*

"This is a book about the stories we write, and perhaps more importantly, the stories we live. It is the most influential work I have yet encountered on the art, nature, and the very purpose of storytelling."
> – Bruce Joel Rubin, Screenwriter, *Stuart Little 2, Deep Impact,*
> *Ghost, Jacob's Ladder*

CHRISTOPHER VOGLER is a veteran story consultant for major Hollywood film companies and a respected teacher of filmmakers and writers around the globe. He has influenced the stories of movies from *The Lion King* to *Fight Club* to *The Thin Red Line* and most recently wrote the first installment of *Ravenskull*, a Japanese-style manga or graphic novel. He is the executive producer of the feature film *P.S. Your Cat is Dead* and writer of the animated feature *Jester Till*.

$26.95 · 300 PAGES · ORDER NUMBER 76RLS · ISBN: 193290736x

THE MYTH OF MWP

In a dark time, a light bringer came along, leading the curious and the frustrated to clarity and empowerment. It took the well-guarded secrets out of the hands of the few and made them available to all. It spread a spirit of openness and creative freedom, and built a storehouse of knowledge dedicated to the betterment of the arts.

The essence of the Michael Wiese Productions (MWP) is empowering people who have the burning desire to express themselves creatively. We help them realize their dreams by putting the tools in their hands. We demystify the sometimes secretive worlds of screenwriting, directing, acting, producing, film financing, and other media crafts.

By doing so, we hope to bring forth a realization of 'conscious media' which we define as being positively charged, emphasizing hope and affirming positive values like trust, cooperation, self-empowerment, freedom, and love. Grounded in the deep roots of myth, it aims to be healing both for those who make the art and those who encounter it. It hopes to be transformative for people, opening doors to new possibilities and pulling back veils to reveal hidden worlds.

MWP has built a storehouse of knowledge unequaled in the world, for no other publisher has so many titles on the media arts. Please visit www.mwp.com where you will find many free resources and a 25% discount on our books. Sign up and become part of the wider creative community!

Onward and upward,

Michael Wiese
Publisher/Filmmaker